Veer Vinayak Damodar Savarkar is a matchless personality of India's movement for freedom. His sacrifice, struggle and indomitable zeal for the freedom, unity and prosperity of the motherland was totally rare, appreciable and exemplary. He plunged himself into the struggle for freedom of the motherland right from his childhood. This path was totally thorny. As a result, he had to face serious difficulties again and again. He was deported to Andamans to undergo two life sentences. Nobody could predict at that time that he would be able to visit his motherland, India, again, but luckily he returned to India ten years later. Terrible physical and mental tortures of Andamans could not deviate him from his call of duty. He did not waver in the face of continuous tortures and reprimands and was always working to realise his objectives. He remained steadfast like the Pole Star.

AF516550

# Veer Vinayak Damodar Savarkar

## An Immortal Revolutionary of India

Bhawan Singh Rana

DIAMOND BOOKS

| | | |
|---|---|---|
| **Publisher** | **:** | **Diamond Pocket Books (P) Ltd.**<br>X-30, Okhla Industrial Area, Phase-II<br>New Delhi-110020 |
| Phone | : | 011-40712200 |
| E-mail | : | sales@dpb.in |
| Website | : | www.dpb.in |
| Edition | : | 2024 |
| Printed by | : | Repro (India) |

**Veer Vinayak Damodar Savarkar : An Immortal Revolutionary of India**
*By : Dr. Bhawan Singh Rana*

# Contents

# Introduction

Veer Vinayak Damodar Savarkar is a matchless personality of India's movement for freedom. His sacrifice, struggle and indomitable zeal for the freedom, unity and prosperity of the motherland was totally rare, appreciable and exemplary. He plunged himself into the struggle for freedom of the motherland right from his childhood. This path was totally thorny. As a result, he had to face difficulties again and again. He was deported to Andamans to undergo two life sentences. Nobody could predict at that time that he would be able to visit his motherland, India, again, but luckily he returned to India ten years later. Terrible physical and mental tortures of Andamans could not deviate him from his call of duty. He did not waver in the face of continuous tortures and reprimands, and was always working to realise his objectives. He remained steadfast like the Pole Star.

His contribution to the freedom of this country was in no way less than of all those political leaders who, after the freedom of India, enjoyed spoils of its administration and power or those who believed in his principles. But it is a matter of both regret and surprise that most of the historians have not evaluated his activities in a just and reasonable manner. Even the government of free India did not accord that respect to this truly dedicated nationalist, indomitably zealous and committed devotee of united India, which he deserved eminently. But this detracts Veer Savarkar from his splendid and high place in history.

Purely idealistic politicians may criticise Savarkar as adversely as they can, but he (Savarkar) remains an ideal to crores and crores of Indians and will continue to inspire in future as well. The purpose of this book is to present as factual as possible a statement of the activities of this great man. An effort has been made to bring in maximum material related to life and philosophy of Veer Savarkar, for

which, besides drawing from the literature of the hero of this book, (acknowledged) assistance has been taken from the books of Shri Shiv Kumar Goyal, Shri Bapu Rao Dharpure, Shri Manmath Nath Gupta and others.

**—Dr. Bhawan Singh Rana**

# Dispute about Veer Savarkar

The countries which want to raise their flag high in the world talk about future and make development plans. We turn the pages of the past and remain embroiled in the disputes of history. The politics of today does not want to miss an opportunity of encashing the great leaders. The dispute in respect of freedom fighter Veer Savarkar assumed such proportions that the work in Parliament came to a standstill. This is not a proper method of a grateful generation, of evaluation of its great leaders. It is pure and simple political hocus-pocus, in which the great leaders are used either as weapons or trump cards. The fresh dispute in respect of Veer Savarkar arose on the issue as to why Central Petroleum Minister Mani Sankar Iyer ordered the removal of the plaque bearing the statement of Veer Savarkar, to be placed below the eternal flame, erected in cellular jail in Andamans and that he should apologise for it. Iyer had said nothing during the formal ceremony, but later on talking to journalists he did not miss the opportunity of expressing his debatable ideas regarding Savarkar. On behalf of the government, Pranab Mukherjee made this clear that the government had nothing to do in the same way with Iyer's statement as the statement of the Prime Minister, in his capacity of the chancellor of Vishwa Bharati, had nothing to do with the government. But the duo of BJP-Shiv Sena are not at all satisfied with this reply.

Savarkar was a freedom fighter. His style of fighting was different. Many leaders like Sukh Dev, Bhagat Singh, Subhash Chandra Bose and *Maharshi* Aurobindo were offering *ahuti* in the *vishal yajna* of freedom. Savarkar was also there, contributing his share.

The previous government under the leadership of Atal

Behari Vajpayee has expressed its respect by installing the picture of Veer Savarkar in the Central Hall of Parliament, despite objections from Congress. And the plaque of Savarkar was placed in the cellular jail with the consent of the earlier Petroleum Minister, which has now been removed on the instructions of the present incumbent, Mr. Iyer. Not only this. He has indicated that the name of the airport there will also be changed. Its name is Veer Savarkar Airport.

Veer Savarkar came out with a tome on the first, *1857 Fight for Freedom.* That book serves as the *Geeta* to the freedom fighters. Many revolutionaries drew inspiration from it in their fight for freedom. Senior Congress leader Vasant Sathe on the occasion of the release of a 10-volume work '*Savarkar Samagra*' on 14 July, 2000 said, "Our head bows with deep respect whenever we mention Batukeshwar Dutt, Bhagat Singh, Chandra Shekhar Azad and Raj Guru. But when we talk of Savarkar, we hesitate, though he inspired and produced hundreds of revolutionaries. The reason for this is that through a well thought out process many misleading things about him have been circulated: To the extent that his name was associated with the murder of Mahatma Gandhi. When Dr. Ambedkar had not even come in sight, Savarkar had established *Patit Pavan Mandir* in Ratnagiri to bring about social equity and harmony.

Indira Gandhi herself had relea ed a postage stamp in the memory of Veer Savarkar. Writing a letter to the secretary of Veer Savarkar National Memorial Committee, she observed, "Veer Savarkar has his own important place in the history of fight for freedom for his daredevilish rebellion against the British government. I wish for success of the birthday celebration of the birth centenary of this brilliant son of India."

She remitted a sum of rupees ten thousand as her contribution to the memorial.

Savarkar suffered for 27 years the tortures of British prisons. The place from where Mani Shankar Iyer has instructed the removal of the flame of freedom, just close to it is that small cellular jail where he underwent solitary confinement of decades.

Rajgopalachari commented, "Savarkar was a national

leader and a symbol of courage, valour and patriotism."

Subhash Chandra Bose wanted that after his release from prison in 1937 he should join the Congress.

When India suffered defeat at the hands of China, General Cariappa said, "If India had listened to Savarkar and adopted the policy of militarization, then we would not have suffered the defeat today."

S.A. Dange, when he was the president of the Communist Party of India, said, "Savarkar was a great revolutionary opposed to colonialism."

Savarkar, undoubtedly, was a great revolutionary, irrespective of the fact that the later half of his life was not that bright and his concept of nationalism was not in conformity with the concept of Indian nation state. But if the public of the country has voted those parties to power, which are the carriers of his line of thinking, and got his symbols respected, then this much of courtesy is required that in future nobody plays with those symbols. If the picture of Savarkar is placed along side of Gandhiji then Savarkar does not become greater than Gandhiji. Why should there be one thought in this country? And why should the right of every one to select one flower out of hundred flowers not be respected? After all, every flower is not a rose. And if you displace or remove other flowers, it neither adds to nor substracts from the glory of the rose.

# Early Life

## Ancestry

Many patriotic great men are born among *Chittapavan Brahmins* of Mharashtra. Balaji Vishwa Nath, the first *Peshwa* of Maratha Empire, Nana Phadanvis, Nana Saheb, the leading commander of India's first fight for freedom, the famous revolutionary Vasu Dev Balwant Phadke, Chafekar brothers, Govind Mahadev Ranade, Gopal Krishna Gokhale, Lokmanya Bal Gangadhar Tilak and others were the progeny of *Chittapavan* line of descent. In the first half of the nineteenth century, one person of this line, Vinayak Dixit lived in Bhagur village of Nasik district, who had two sons, Mahadev and Damodar.

Damodar Pant Savarkar studied upto Matriculation and on completion of his studies he became a teacher in a school in a nearby village. He was married at an early age of eighteen as per tradition of the times. His life-partner Radha Bai was just a ten-year-old innocuous girl at that time. Both husband and wife were religious minded persons in the family. Lord Ram and Krishna were their favourite gods and Durga, riding a lion, was their Kul Devi. The family atmosphere was thoroughly replete with ideas of Hinduism.

## Birth and Childhood

A child was born to this Savarkar couple on *Vaishakh Krishna* 6 of *Samvat* 1940, i.e. 28th May, 1883, who later on was known as Veer Vinayak Damodar Savarkar in the history of India. It is said that, when he was just a few months old, he used to cry so much that sometimes he would abandon suckling at his mother's breasts. Once he was crying continuously and unconsolably and nobody knew what to do. He was, at that time, cradled in the arms of his *Tauji*, Mahadev Savarkar. He tried his level best, but the baby would not stop crying. All of a sudden words gushed out of his *Tauji's* lips, "If you are the incarnation of your ancestor, Vinayak Dixit, we will give you that name. O.K. Now calm down and take milk." After saying this he put a mark (*Tilak*) of ashes on the forehead of the baby. Surprise of all surprises. The baby stopped crying and took his milk. He was named Vinayak after the name of his grand father. The name of the father is also written along with son's name as per tradition in South India, and so he was called Vinayak Damodar Savarkar.

Veer Vinayak Savarkar, the main character of this book, were five brothers and two sisters, out of whom two brothers and one sister died quite early. Vinayak Savarkar was second among surviving brothers and sisters. Shri Ganesh Savarkar was his elder brother, and Maina his younger sister, and Narayan Savarkar his younger brother. It has already been mentioned that Savarkar's mother Radha Bai and father Damodar Savarkar both were highly religious minded Hindus. Besides telling stories from the *Ramayana* and the *Mahabharata*, both the parents narrated to their children the courageous legends of great men of history such as *Maharana* Pratap, *Guru* Govind Singh and *Chhatrapati* Shivaji. Child Savarkar soaked it all in. He developed a respectful feeling for Hinduism in his heart right from childhood. He began dreaming of establishing a Hindu nation. This feeling took roots and strengthened itself in his later life.

Vinayak was lovingly called Tatya in his family. He was just nine years old when his mother passed away in 1892. It was an unbearable blow to child Vinayak. Later, his father played the role of his mother also for him. The job of worship of *Kul Devi* Durga was left to child Tatya by his highly religious father.

Near about this time in 1893-95 Hindu-Muslim riots erupted all over the country. This gave rise to love for his community in the heart of child Tatya. In 1897, Poona was engulfed in a fury of plague. In the guise of preventing plague, the Britishers entered houses and misbehaved with the inmates. All the residents of Poona were infuriated by the misconduct of a British officer, named Mr. Rand. *Lok*

*Manya* Tilak wrote articles opposing him in his paper *Kesari.*

This year, on 22nd June the Diamond Jubilee of Queen Victoria's coronation was also being celebrated. A ceremony was going on in Poona also. Chafekar brothers could not bear the continuance of the ceremony amidst this miserable condition of the country. They killed Mr. Rand and Earst.

On 12t June, 1897 the coronation of Shivaji was celebrated. On this occasion, Tilak came out with some articles praising Shivaji and justifying some of his actions. *Lok Manya* Tilak was charged with supporting the political assassination of Rand, and he was sentenced to jail. All this cycle of events helped sprouting of love for his country in the heart of child Tatya. He desired a quick destination of the British rule.

Vinayak had to face another serious blow nearly two years after these happenings. In 1899 his father Damodar Pant also died of plague. After his father's death, the responsibility for the whole family devolved on his elder brother, Ganesh Savarkar. He took both of his younger brothers and sister and came to Nasik. Ganesh Savarkar was married. With his wife, Yashoda, he started looking after his younger brothers and sister in a loving and caring way.

Ganesh Savarkar discharged his duty towards his younger brothers, after the death of their father, in a proper and comprehensive manner. It was the result of his carefully managed efforts that there was no disturbance in the studies of Vinayak Savarkar. Vinayak also saw the image of his parents in his brother and sister-in-law all through his life. When he was studying for his matriculation, Vinayak was also married. His wife was the daughter of Bhau Saheb Chiplunkar. His married life did not distract him in any way in his studies and love for the country. On the other hand, we see that his life-partner inspired him always towards an ideal and discharge of duty in life.

**Education**

Child Tatya was admitted to the village school for his primary education in 1889. He studied in this school upto 5th standard. In this primary stage of his education, child

Tatya played battle-related games with boys of his age. Two groups of students were formed; artificial forts were also made. Then one group attacked the other.

He was sent to Nasik to pursue his studies further, after he had passed in 5th standard in this village school. In his student life also, Tatya's love for his country continued to grow. He taught his friends and class fellows here also love for their country. He started writing poems also in Marathi during this school period. His poems, filled with patriotism, were published in the main Marathi magazines and newspapers of the day. Additionally, he was drawn towards the study of patriotic literature as well. Reading newspapers with patriotic and nationalistic slant became the main activity of his life.

Savarkar passed his matriculation examination in 1901. Later on, he became a student of Fergusson College, Poona, for higher studies. Here, too, he formed a group of like-minded youths, and started teaching and inspiring them with patriotism.

### Activities Other than Studies during Student Life

When Vinayak Savarkar got admission in Fergusson College in 1902, the Principal was Sir Jadunath Pranjape, a scholar of Mathematics. On getting admission in this college, he was highly pleased to realise that he would get an opportunity to put his ideas across to people. Through his writings and lectures, in a very short span of time, he became a well-known person not only in the college but in the city as well. Here he came in contact with *Lok-manya* Tilak whose inspiration nourished his love for the country. He stayed in the college hostel when he was studying here. In the hostel the students themselves managed the mess. In Savarkar they found a good manager for this work. Discussions on political movements were a regular feature in the hostel room in which he lived. One student or the other was always present and discussing there. So his room came to be known as Savarkar Camp.

Savarkar had made many good friends as one Mr. Khaparde in Deccan College, Poona also. So the meetings related to movements were held either in Deccan College or on a hillock opposite Fergusson College.

Savarkar started bringing out a paper also as soon as he was admitted to Fergusson College. It was a hand-written paper. Besides studies, he took active part in debates and other cultural activities also. History was his most favourite subject. He had a deep knowledge of not only Indian history, but that of the whole world. During his student life, once a debate was held in his college about history of Italy. Savarkar also participated in this debate. The then Principal of the college was thoroughly surprised on hearing his lecture. The Principal himself taught history, but on hearing the lecture of Savarkar he acknowledged in the most clear words that, though reading and teaching of history was his 24-hour job, his (Savarkar's) knowledge of history was more extensive, comprehensive and superior.

**Poems Replete with Nationalistic Sentiments**

Vinayak Savarkar was writing poems replete with nationalistic sentiments right from his early student life. The themes of these poems (*Povari*) were freedom-loving heroes of history, such as *Maharana* Pratap, *Chhatrapati* Shivaji, *Guru* Govind Singh et al. He instilled nationalistic feelings in his friends through these poems full of courage and bravery. At one place in these *povaris* it is stated about a cousin brother (Baji Ghorpade who was a supporter of *Sultan* Bajipur) of Shivaji, "Oh My! My! Brave Baji Prabhu is in the service of *Yavan* (Muslim) Sultan. He is helping a foreigner of different religion for the slavery of our motherland."

Further ahead in the poem, a messenger of Shivaji goes to Baji and tells him, "O Baji! Why do you co-operate with that low butcher of a different rleigion for the slavery of our motherland? Fie on the person who doesn't love self-rule and his country. This is not the defect of religion that base (*mlechcha*) people are strong today. We have a whole *bazar* of traitorous *chandals*. Brave Baji! Why are you wasting away your life in this slavery? Shivaji, the incarnation of Lord Shankar, defender of cows and *Brahmins* and consolidator of freedom, is calling you. He is invoking you to join the fight for freedom. Go there, and repent after drinking the *amrit* of patriotism. Be a commander of freedom loving army."

The message has the desired impact on Baji. He is disgusted with his activities. He tells the messenger, "Mistaking a highly venomous snake as my friend, I have given him shelter in my house. I acknowledged this anti-Hindu thief, this foreigner of a different religion as my king, and opposed the highly valorous Shivaji. I became the servant of the man who is defiling our pious motherland. O messengers! Go and tell Shivaji *Maharaj* that he cuts into pieces a treacherous person like me. I want to take a re-birth in this pious land, after being killed—freed at the hands of freedom loving Hindu brave man, Shivaji."

First poem of Savarkar was published in 1894. His poems were published in Marathi magazines. *Lok-manya* Tilak and Govind Mahadev Ranade came to know of him through these poems. They extended their good wishes to Savarkar for these poems. Later on the government seized these poems, declaring them as abetment of people against the government. In a magazine of Nasik, *Nasik Vaibhav*, an article of Savarkar, entilled '*Hindustan Gaurav*' was published, which was highly praised by all his teachers.

**Mitra Mela**

Chafekar brothers founded *Hindu Dharma Sanrakshini Sabha* in 1894. Chafekar brothers were hanged to death in the case of murder of Mr. Rand, described earlier. This hanging roused strong anger against the Britishers in the whole country. This incident made Vinayak Savarkar a sworn enemy of the Britishers, and he took a pledge before his *Kul Devi* to continue life-long struggle for the freedom of his motherland. He formed *Mitra Mela* of students in order to redeem this pledge. He started organising '*Shivaji Mahotsava*', '*Ganesh Mahotsava*' under the auspices of *Mitra Mela*. In these celebrations youths were trained for armed revolution. Very soon a large number of youths became its members, impressed by the lectures of Savarkar. When Queen Victoria passed away on 22nd January, 1901, many condolence meetings were held all over India. Savarkar could not bear this sycophancy and mental slavery.

Expressing his opposition to condolence meetings, he said in a meeting of *Mitra Mela*: "The queen of England is a queen of a country which is our enemy. So why should we mourn? To mourn the death of a queen who shackled us in chains of slavery will demonstrate our slavish mentality only."

All the activities of *Mitra Mela*, like the activities of *Hindu Dharma Sanrakshini Sabha*, began with verses in praise of Lord Ganesh and Shivaji. In these verses, the listeners were enjoined upon to lay down their lives for the freedom of the motherland as Shivaji did. For instance, "Friends! We pledge to lay down our lives in the battlefield for our nation. We will colour the earth red with the blood of those people who are destroying our religion and our motherland, or are harming them in any form. We will die only after killing all our enemies."

**Bonfire of Foreign Clothes**

In 1905, when Savarkar was preparing for his B.A. (Final) examination, he decided to discard foreign clothes. Moderate Congress leaders were of a clear opinion that the results of this decision would not be good or useful. Indians will have to face the opposition of the government, peace-loving public and Anglo-Indians. On the other hand, hawks in the Congress wanted that the youths should undertake the publicity work of *swadeshi* (indigenous) goods, and that, instead of making bonfire of foreign clothes, they should be distributed among the poor. Savarkar was very clear in his views and held that in order to rouse strong anger in public against the government, it was essential that foreign clothes were burnt collectively. Therefore, on 22nd August, 1906, they publically held a bonfire of foreign clothes in Poona for the first time. *Lokmanya* Tilak himself presided over this function. The news of this courageous act of Savarkar flashed through the whole world. This incident continued to be an issue of discussion of newspapers also for some time. He was expelled from his college as a consequence of this incident. Later on, he was permitted to appear for B.A. from Bombay University. He passed his B.A. from there.

The Principal of Fergusson College imposed on him a fine of ten rupees, being unhappy with his inflammatory lectures, before the bonfire of foreign clothes. *Lok-manya* Tilak opposed this fine through the medium of *Kesari*. When the friends and well-wishers of Savarkar heard of the imposition of fine, they remitted to him money more than the amount of fine. Savarkar donated the extra amount for the publicity of *swadeshi* goods. From here onwards, he became the most dangerous man for the government.

**Abhinav Bharat**

After passing his B.A., Savarkar organised a forum, named *Abhinav Bharat* in a secret meeting. The aim of this organisation was to train youths for an armed revolution. A youth had to take the following vow before obtaining a membership of this organisation.

"In the name of Chhatrapati Shivaji, in the name of my pious religion, and in the name of my dear country, and taking a pledge in the name of my ancestors I vow to continue to struggle till my last breath for complete freedom of my nation. I'll neither laze about nor step back from my objective. I'll fully comply with the rules of *Abhinav Bharat* and will maintain total secrecy about the activities and programmes of the organisation."

Savarkar moved from place to place to motivate and organise young men for this objective. His speeches were highly patriotic and brilliant when he undertook this task. Some extracts from his speeches are as follows:

"O Children of Chhatrapati Shivaji! You have to establish an independent Hindu empire after crushing the atrocious British empire which shackles mother India in chains of slavery in the same way as Shivaji destroyed the Moghul empire, and as Sadashiv Rao Bhau smashed the Maghul throne. We have to overthrow this foreign empire through armed struggle and revolution."

In India ceremonies were being held all over to celebrate the coronation of Edward the VIIth. Savarkar considered those Indians as supporters of slavery, who were expressing happiness on the coronation of an emperor who was enslaving the country. So he came out with a poster to express his strong anger. In this poster, he wrote, "O Indians! You are celebrating the coronation of a king who has enslaved your motherland. This festival will be a festival of slavery."

**In Contact with Paramhansa, an Inaccessible Guru**

In 1905, Savarkar came in contact with a Mahatma, whose name was *Agamya Guru Paramhansa.* Paramhansa had travelled all over India and lectured at different places. He spoke against the government in these lectures and asked people not to be afraid of it. He formed a committee of nine persons in Poona, most of whom had been students of Fergusson College. This committee had collected some money also for activities to be undertaken. It seems that when Vinayak Savarkar went to England, the committee was disbanded. Then some of its members joined '*Tarun Bharat Sabha*,' an outfit organised by Ganesh Savarkar, the elder brother of Vinayak. So Vinayak Savarkar remained in contact with Guru Paramhansa for a very short time.

Before leaving for London, Savarkar toured through all big cities of Maharashtra. In this itinerary, he discussed the subject of the freedom of the country with his revolutionary friends, and delivered speeches at different places to awaken people. A big meeting was organised in his honour, in which good wishes for his studies in London were expressed. After this, he became busy with preparations for his departure to London.

# Activities in London

### Departure

Savarkar wanted to go to England to complete his course of Law (Barrister), after passing his B.A. But finance was the main problem before him. His father-in-law Bhau Rao Chiplunkar gave him a thousand rupees, but this amount could not solve his problem. These days Pandit Shyamji Krishna Verma, stationed in London, was directing revolutionaries for India's freedom. He had founded India House in London and was publishing a paper '*Indian Sociologist*'. He had arranged some scholarships also for Indian students studying in London. *Lokmanya* Tilak wrote a letter to Vermaji for arranging a scholarship for Savarkar. So Savarkar got a scholarship. Thus, finding a solution for his financial problem, he left for London on 9th June, 1906 from Bombay Port. *Lokmanya* Tilak himself came to the port to see him off.

### Activities of Savarkar in England

Savarkar stayed in India House of Shyamji Krishna Verma on reaching London. Verma helped him here in all possible ways. India House was a centre of patriots, so Savarkar found himself in an environment that 'suited his thinking'. A few days after reaching London he founded 'Free India Society'. Patriotic young men like Bhai Parmanand, Madan Lal Dhingra, Harnam Singh, Koregaonkar, and Lala Har Dayal became its members. In meetings of this society, its members thought and discussed about the freedom of India. In its first meeting, Savarkar, in his speech, said, "The British empire in India can be brought to an end if Indian youths, with arms in their hands, are ready and committed to die and killing. India's freedom is possible only though armed revolution. We have to prepare Indian youths for this. We have to help them with arms." Along with this, he continued to advance in London the activities of 'Abhinav Bharat'. Before he reached London, the work of India's freedom was carried out only through the medium of newspapers. Savarkar pledged to change this completely.

### '1857 Ka Swatantrya Samar', a Great Work

Savarkar left India to become a barrister, but he accorded primacy to the study of history on reaching here. He frequented the university very little. He spent most of his time in the British Library. He was impressed by the brave man of Italy, Mezzini, and wrote his biography, and in 1906 he came out with a book *Sfurtidayak Itihas*, of Sikhs. After this, delving further deep in history, he came out with a tome, *1857 Ka Swatantrya Samar.*

British historians had dubbed the 1857 fight for freedom as a rebellion, loot and mutiny and, therefore, of no significance, but Savarkar by writing this book proved that it was India's first fight for freedom, fought by India's brave sons for the freedom of their motherland, and he gave compelling evidence in support of his opinion. This book was first written in Marathi in 1907. Later on Savarkar read out its important parts in English translation. As soon as the news reached the Britishers, they proscribed it and ordered its seizure, but the manuscript of the book was very secretly sent to India. Attempts were made to get it published in India, but the police raided printers and the book could not be published, and it was sent back to Savarkar. Its first English translation was published from Holland. The British government had already declared it illegal. Therefore, thousands of its copies were sent to France. Some copies were sent to India and other countries. The book became very popular among the revolutionaries. Later on the publication of its second edition was organised by Madam Bhikaji Cama and Lala Har Dayal. After this, Bhagat Singh also got it published secretly. Its single copy was sold for rupees three hundred each, at that time, because the book was so well received.

In 1907, Savarkar celebrated in London the half century

of India's first fight for freedom. Youths wore badges inscribed '*1857 ke Shahidon ki Jai*'. Giving vent to their contempt, the British teachers called the martyrs of this struggle as dacoits and looters. Youths got into argument with them on this. As a consequence, the students boycotted the university. All the main newspapers of the world debated the issue. These incidents made the police in England more alert. Therefore, every activity of Savarkar was watched. He wrote articles in support of our freedom struggle and got them published all over the world. Many English journalists supported him, as a consequence of the impact of these articles.

When Shyamji Krishna Verma went to France, Savarkar directed India House efficiently. He sent Sardar Singh Rana and Madam Bhikaji Cama as India's representative to International Socialists' Conference in Germany, where for the first time Madam Cama unfurled a flag with *Vande Mataram* written on it.

Savarkar despatched two youths to Russian revolutionaries to learn how to make a bomb. Later on these two young men were sent to India, with some pistols and a book dealing with the method of making a bomb.

**Publicity of Revolution among Indian Soldiers**

Savarkar wanted to publicise revolution among Indian soldiers. For this, be collected the home addresses of Sikh, Jat and Dogra soldiers, and sent letters to them twice or thrice a month to inspire and prepare them for revolution. When these letters were ready, Sikh youths translated them into Hindi and Punjabi. They were printed with the help of a duplicator on wax-paper and despatched. This activity continued for many months unhindered. Later on, the secret was leaked out. Therefore, the soldiers were ordered that reading or keeping of such letters would be considered an offence, and whosoever had those letters should surrender them to his officers. When the secret was out, Savarkar stopped despatching those letters. Sardar Ajit Singh (uncle of Bhagat Singh) got lakhs of copies of these letters printed in India and distributed them all over the country.

### Birth Anniversary of Lord Ram in England

Savarkar considered Lord Ram as an ideal for all human beings. That is why on the birth anniversary of Lord Ram, he said:

"If I were the dictator of this country, then I would first of all order the seizure the *Ramayana* written by Valmiki, because so long as the Hindus have this scripture in their hands, till then neither can Hindus bow their heads to any other God or emperor, nor can their tribe be destroyed... The *Ramayana* is the original scripture of democracy, a scripture which is not only the story of democracy, it is its sentry, inspirer and producer as well. So long as it is there, no dictator can come up there. Is there any emperor, incarnation or prophet who can stand before Ram?"

Indian youths were stirred to their depths to attain freedom on listening to these brilliant lectures.

### Sacrifices of Dhingra

Madan Lal Dhingra had come to London from Punjab for studies. He became ready to serve his motherland after coming in contact with Savarkar. He expressed his desire to Savarkar. To test him, Savarkar stabbed him in his hand with a knife, but Dhingra did not wince or utter anything. So he was taken as a disciple. 'India Office' under the presidentship of Curzon Wylie was established to control the revolutionary activities of Indian youths in England. Apparently this institution demonstrated sympathy towards Indians, but its objective was to spy on Indian revolutionaries. After becoming the disciple of Savarkar, Madan Lal Dhingra went to Curzon Wylie and became a member of India Office. His friends started looking upon him as a traitor, but Dhingra had something else in his mind. On 1st July, 1909 he shot Curzon Wylie dead in the Jehangir Hall of Imperial Institute. So be was taken a prisoner.

This incident created a hallaballo all around. Dhingra's father felt threatened. By sending a telegram, he declared that he had nothing to do with his son. Meetings were held in India condemning this murder. In London also, Indians held a meeting. All were condemning the action of Dhingra, in the end as the chairman of the meeting rose to declare a unanimous resolution of condemnation (according to Manmath Nath Gupta the meeting was chaired by Vipin Pal, but according to Shiv Kumar Goyal, Savarkar's biographer, Agha Khan was the chairman of the meeting) Savarkar thundered and opposed the resolution. He said that the case of Dhingra was sub-judice and, therefore, any such activity could influence the case. Where everybody was speaking in one tone, the Britishers, present there, were cut to the quick by this unexpected opposition. An Englishman, saying, "O.K. enjoy a British punch, and see how well it suits", gave a punch to Savarkar, bitting him in the eye. His spects were broken and blood started flowing from his eye. Before that Englishman could balance himself after giving that punch, an Indian youth, M.T.T. Acharya, saying, "savour this as well, it is Indian *danda* (stick)" struck a blow with stick on the head of that Englishman, which wounded him. As a consequence the resolution of condemnation could not be adopted. Savarkar was arrested, but in the absence of evidence, he was released soon

Admitting his crime in the court, Dhingra said, "I have tried to take a very ordinary revenge from the blood of this Englishman, of the inhuman hangings and deportations of hundreds of our patriots at the hands of the Britishers. I have not consulted anybody except my own discretion in this respect....my only prayer to God is to allow me to take birth from the same mother and sacrifice my life for the same pious objective. I will continue to wish this so long as India does not attain freedom. I'll wish so that the well-being of humanity is accomplished and God's grace and empire expands. *Vande Mataram.*"

The court at West Minster sentenced Dhingra to death, and he was hanged on 16th August, 1909. Prior to this Savarkar met him in Bristol jail and said, "I have come for your *darshan.*"

Paying tributes to Dhingra after his hanging, Savarkar said, "The statement of martyr Dhingra is a valuable, worth mentioning proof of the purpose of the Revolutionaries... Dhingra was a highly self-respecting Hindu. In his opinion, the murder of the enemy of our nation was in line with the courageous tradition of self-respecting Hindus like Lord Ram, Krishna, Shivaji, Pratap and others. It was a Godly act. It was a trumpet, a spark igniting the flame of India's fight for freedom, his statement."

**Arrested**

After the above mentioned incident the police in England was after Savarkar, hammer and tongs. Therefore, his friends advised him to go to Paris. He went to Paris. But his heart was not here. Though Shyamji Krishna Verma was in Paris these days and he advised Savarkar to stay there, but he did not agree and came back to England. As soon as he reached London on 13th March, 1910, he was arrested. He was charged with the following:

1. Conspiracy against the British government in India.
2. To destroy the sovereignty of the British Emperor.
3. Collection and distribution of illegal arms and inciting youths to murder Jackson and Curzon Wylie.
4. Collection of arms in London and their export to India.
5 Treasonous speeches in London and India.

In the background of these charges, it will not be irrelevant to have a look at the incidents in India, the arrest of Ganesh Savarkar and Narayan Savarkar for Jackson's murder and other similar incidents. Prior to the arrest of Vinayak Savarkar, his elder brother Ganesh Savarkar got a collection of poems, entitled *Laghu Abhinav Bharat Mela* published in 1908. The government considered these poems inciting and provocative and a case was instituted against him under Section 121. As a consequence on 9th June, 1909 he was deported (to Andamans) for life. Judge Jackson had tried this case in a lower court. So on 21st December 1909, a 16-year-old young man Kanhere shot Jackson dead during his farewell party. It is said that the pistol used for this murder was sent by Savarkar from London, which has been mentioned earlier. Seven persons were tried in Jackson's murder case, and three of them including Kanhere were hanged.

The information of his elder brother's sentence was sent to Savarkar in London. It is said that on receiving this information he shouted at India House and loudly said that it would be avenged.

Sometime after this, his younger brother Narayan Savarkar was also arrested. He was charged with being involved in revolutionary activities. On receiving this information, Savarkar felt proud of his brothers, and as if involuntarily, he gushed forth: "Fine. Well what more glory can we have than this that all of us (three brothers) are immersed in the worship of *Swatantraya Shree* (splendour of freedom)!"

On the arrest of his elder brother, Savarkar wrote a consoling letter to his sister-in-law, which was in the form of a poem. A brief meaning of the lines is presented here below:

"The lotus flower offered by Gajendra at the feet of the Lord, though uprooted from its soil, becomes immortal. In the same we all three brothers will attain *moksha* (salvation) by dedicating ourselves at the feet of motherland."

Savarkar wrote again to his respected sister-in-law from Bristol jail. It was in Marathi, and was in the nature of his last testament, because he had understood that he would be hanged. Some of the lines of this letter ran like this:

"Motherland! I have placed my heart at your feet. My speeches, beauty of expression, my new poem—everything is dedicated at your feet...our lineage may or may not continue, but, O Motherland! Bless us to fulfil our objectives. We feel grateful at having burnt everything we had, in the fire we built for removing the chains and shackles of mother. *Pujya Bhabhi!* Consider, the success of our lineage is in this. Parvati has performed *tapa* on the peaks of the Himalayas and many Rajput queens and princesses have laid down their lives smiling. That glory and strength of Indian women has not been destroyed yet..."

**Jumping into the Sea**

When Savarkar was arrested and lodged into Bristol jail, his friends thought that he would be tried in London. Perhaps, the British government feared that this might give a tool in the hands of Savarkar to blast the British justice. It was also possible that he was effortlessly catapulted into fame. So it was decided to take him to India and try him there. When Savarkar came to know of this decision of the British government, he sent the following message to Indian revolutionaries active there:

"Just as all the living or dead actors of an Indian drama appear on the stage and meet in the end, in the same way, we all innumerable actors of this drama of struggle (for freedom) will at one time or other meet at the stage of history, and our audience in the form of humanity will welcome us happily. Friends! So long! Bye, Bye.

"My dead body may fall anywhere, whether in the solitary cell in Andamans or in the most pious stream of Ganga, it will impart an impetus alone to our struggle. Fighting and falling in battle is also a kind of success. So, dear friends! Bye, Bye!"

On 1st July, 1910 a ship named Moria look Veer Savarkar on board and sailed from England to India. There was strict guard in the ship.

On the other side in Paris, revolutionaries like Shyamji Krishna Verma, Lala Har Dayal et al. had planned to get Savarkar freed when the ship reached the French port. Savarkar knew this. It was decided that on reaching here, Savarkar would jump from the ship into the sea and a taxi would take him to Paris.

The ship, Moria, carrying Savarkar reached Marseilles port of France on 8th July, 1910. Savarkar went to toilet, and therein holding to its window jumped into the sea. His guards stood helpless. They warned and fired, but Savarkar did not care for it. He kept swimming and reached the shore. These was a high wall facing him. He tried to climb it, but fell down. He tried again, and with great difficulty succeeded in climbing it and landed on the French soil. He started running. In the meanwhile his guards, too, reached there in boats. Shyamji Krishna Verma and other revolutionaries were late by just fifteen minutes. The French police, ignoring and flouting international rules, arrested and handed him over to the police of England. Unfortunately this attempt did not succeed. The news of this sensational incident spread through the whole world like electricity.

All newspapers published it prominently and condemned the actions of the French police.

**Savarkar in International Court**

To come to the land of a free nation, France, and to forcibly take away a free citizen was an international offence. Enlightened French citizens criticised this act of the British police and put pressure on their government to bring Savarkar back. At that time France and England were coming close together in self-defence against Germany, so the French government could not apply adequate pressure on the British government. So both the countries handed the case over to International Court of Justice at the Hague.

The first sitting of the court was held on 16th February, 1911. Later on 24th February itself the Court decided that there was no need to hand over Veer Savarkar to France. This biased judgement, too, was criticised throughout the world.

**Drama of Justice in India**

Veer Savarkar was lodged in Yervada jail after being bought to India. The government constituted a special court to try him. It had three judges—Sir Basil Scott (Chief Judge), Sir N.G. Chandravarkar, and Heaton. Shyamji Krishna Verma and Madam Cama engaged the famous British advocate Mr. Joseph Baptista to plead on his behalf. In addition to Baptista, Shri Govind Rao Gadgil, Shri Ranganekar and Shri Chitre voluntarily helped Veer Savarkar.

Two cases were instituted against him:

1. Conspiracy, with 36 other persons, against the British emperor.
2. Abetment to murder Jackson, collector of Nasik.

The cast started in Bombay on 15th December, 1910. His advocate Joseph Baptista, by moving an application, submitted and stated in the court that the arrest was illegally effected from the land of France. Therefore, the case should be adjourned till this issue is resolved, but this prayer was rejected.

**Two Life Sentences**

The court awarded life sentence to Veer Savarkar and seizure of his property on 24th December, 1910 under section 121 A for abetment to people to rebel against the British government and for training people in making bombs etc. 25 other youths were also along with him awarded sentences of imprisonment for varied periods.

After the first case, the second one relating to the murder of Jackson started on 23rd January, 1911, and within a week, on 30th January, its judgement was also pronounced. In this judgement also he was again awarded life sentence. Pronouncing the judgement, Chief Judge Basil Scott categorically said, "A ferocious (convict) criminal like Savarkar should undergo two life sentences, i.e. deported for 50 years."

Award of two life sentences was definitely unprecedented. It sent a wave of anxiety and anger across India. Indians wrote thousands of letters to the government protesting awards to Veer Savarkar, but they did not result into any thing positive.

# In Andamans

Veer Savarkar was kept in Dongri jail after the award of two life sentences, before being deported to Andamans. Here the work of pounding coconut shells to prepare staples for ropes was assigned to him. One day Mrs. Mai, his wife, reached this jail to see him; she was just nineteen at this time. Tears came to her eyes on seeing her husband in this condition. Veer Savarkar consoled and encouraged his wife, demonstrating his exemplary valour. Playing the role of an ideal husband, he said, "Don't worry. With the grace of God, I will certainly meet you again. However consider this. If world life means rearing sons and daughters and making a home by collecting a few straws, then the birds and crows also set up a nest, home for themselves. But if the liberal meaning of family is human family, then we have certainly succeded in rearing that family. Agreed that we have destroyed a happy life with our own hands. But in future happiness will rain in thousands of homes. Shall we not find our sacrifice relevant then? Many people dreaming of a happy world become victims of plague, and their homes are rendered dark and lampless. Death snatches husbands and wives away from the *mandap* of marriage. So learn to face adversities and keep patience."

Mrs. Mai, though outwordly fragile, was internally strong. Demonstrating her mettle, she said, "You need not worry. Is it a matter of lesser happiness to me that my brave husband is undergoing the most rigorous discipline and dedication in the service of motherland?"

From Dongri Jail, Savarkar was taken to Byculla jail, and was made to perform most rigorous tasks as in earlier jail. Describing the sufferings in this jail, he wrote, "The cell in Thane prison, to which I was confined, had the most notorious Muslim warders. Totally alone. Food was served. I could not swallow a single morsel. Stale and useless *chapati* of millet (*bajra*). A strange, sour vegetable.

Difficult to place in mouth. A piece of *chapati* was taken, slightly chewed. A draught of water, and then swallow it down with water."

One day the warder informed him that his younger brother Dr. Narayan Damodar Savarkar was also lodged in the same jail. 20 years old Narayan Savarkar was arrested on charges of throwing bomb on Lord Minto. It is to be remembered that his elder brother Ganesh Damodar Savarkar had already been deported to Andamans to undergo his sentence.

Veer Savarkar sent a letter to his younger brother through that warder. He advised his brother in this letter not to waver or get perturbed in the face of difficulties: "You need not worry at all for me, or make yourself sad on that account. If using body as a fuel one has to burn in order to provide steam of inspiration to others, why should we not get that role? To keep on burning is also an activity. Not merely this, it is a great activity."

Needless to say that Narayan Savarkar got ideal self-confidence and strength from this letter.

Veer Savarkar lived in these jails for about four months after the judgement from the court.

**Departure to Andamans**

Four months after his confinement in the above mentioned jails, a ship named *Maharaja* took him to Andamans and reached there on 4th July, 1911. The jailor of Andaman jail was an Irishman, named Barie. As soon as he saw Savarkar, he said, "If you tried to escape as you did at Marseilles, you'll get into very great trouble. There are dense forests around the jail, where in fierce tribals and foresters live. They eat youths like you as cucumber."

On hearing this, Savarkar said, "Immediately on my arrest, I have studied the history of my future residence, Andamans. Therefore, you need not tell me more about this."

**Prisoner's Life in Andamans**

Veer Vinayak Savarkar was lodged in 123rd cell of

barrack no. 7 of Andaman jail. Serious offenders (of India) convicted of murder, dacoity etc. were lodged here. Alongside, the political prisoners, who were sentenced for life, were also sent here. Here, the life of the prisoner was of the lowest order, and the conduct of jailor, warder etc. was entirely in- human. Veer Savarkar, describing his early days here, wrote:

"*Jamadar* look me to barrack No. 7. There was a tank of water on the way. *Jamadar* said, 'Take your bath here'. I had not taken my bath, for many days. Body was dirty with sweating and for not having taken a bath. So as soon as I was permitted to take bath. I feel happy in an unprecedented way. I was given a *langot* (underwear) to wear while bathing. On wearing *langot* as I tried to take water in a bowl, the *jamadar* shouted, 'Don't do this. This is *Kala Pani*. When I order you to take water, you will bend and take one bowl of water. When I say 'rub your parts of body' then you rub your parts with this water. When I ask you to take more water, you will take two more bowls of water. Thus, you will take your bath in three bowls of water only."

"As per habit, when I took little water in my mouth for *kulla*, the brackish water spoiled the entire taste of the tongue. The whole body jerked spasmodically. Thought, it would have been letter if I did not take bath. But then thought again, 'I'll have to get used to it.' If I have enjoyed the Turkish bath in London and Parisian bath, I should enjoy the Andamanish bath also."

Next morning the Pathan warder of the jail came running to Savarkar, and said, "Stand, Saheb is coming." Savarkar stood near the bars of the door. Just then jailor Barie came there along with a few more whites. He started discussion to prove 1857 fight for freedom as mutiny. Savarkar stood his ground, offered compelling evidence and proved that it was a fight for freedom.

In jail the prisoners were treated in a totally inhuman way. The conduct of jailor Barie was that of a completely uncivilised man. If another co-prisoner addressed Savarkar as *Babu*, then he (Barie) immediately shouted at him and said, "which *sala* is *babu* here? Here all are *sale* prisoners." He was not prepared even to accept Savarkar as a political prisoner. He was assigned ward 'D', which he had to wear on his clothes.

**Inhuman Tortures**

Prisoners were asked to pound coconut shell and take staple out of it. The prisoners talked among themselves while doing this work. Once an officer from Calcutta came to visit the jail. He could not bear that the prisoners talked among themselves. It was ordered that the work should be extracted from prisoners with greater strictness. So, they were harnessed in oil expellers (*kolhus*). If they talked among themselves, they were handcuffed for a week. While harnessing them in oil expellers, the health of the political prisoners was not taken into consideration. The prisoners ran the oil expellers in the closed cells. They were taken out at the time of food. They were not allowed even to wash their hands. If they washed their hands or stood in the sun for a few minutes, then *numberdar* showered filthy abuses on them (reflecting badly on their mothers and sisters). Prisoners had to fawn on them for drinking water also. They got only two bowlful of water, not the third. They could not take their bath, except when it rained. Immediately after getting their food, they were sent back to their cells and closed shut. No one bothered whether a prisoner ate his food or not. As soon as they were back in their cells, a voice from outside warned, "Don't sit. We should get complete oil in the evening. Otherwise you will be beaten. Other punishment will follow, additionally."

Often, the prisoners ate their food while remaining harnessed in the oil expellers. If the oil extracted was less, they were beaten with sticks, punches and kicks as you do with animals. Barie, the jailor, did not allow any relaxation, if one ran a fever upto 102°F. If a prisoner complained of stomach-ache or headache, which were not visible, he was treated/beaten so severely that he would lose his shape. On a complaint from the prisoner, the doctor used thermometer for temperature, but he could not measure pain, as it was immeasurable. The doctor was a Hindu. Barie misbehaved with him also and said, "Doctor! See. You are a Hindu. These political prisoners are also Hindus. I wonder if their sweet talks don't sour your job here. I fear it. If somebody reported that you are talking with them, it will be extremely harmful to you. Therefore, take care. You understand! Take care of your job! I know you have studied medicine, but we are also experienced. Who is really ill, and who is not, I know immediately in a glance."

Veer Savarkar's elder brother, Ganesh Savarkar, was also in this jail. Once he had a horrible headache. The doctor permitted him to be taken to the hospital. All formalities for taking him to hospital had also been completed. He was being taken to hospital. Just then Barie reached there, and soon got angry. "Why didn't you consult me? Who is that doctor? You son-of-a-bitch, take him back. Put him to work. I'll deal with the doctor. Why did you take him out of the cell without my permission? You damn! Am I the jailor or that doctor is the jailor?" As a result the patient could not be taken to hospital.

Besides this abusing, manhandling, senseless beating and miserliness regarding food and clothes, the prisoners did not have freedom to attend to their calls of nature (i.e. going to toilet or for passing urine). Except in the morning, evening and noontime, the prisoners were not allowed to go out to attend to calls of nature. If during the night they discharged urine or passed stool, they had to face the sanitary workers in the morning, and they were presented to officers to explain their conduct. They were handcuffed standing, and had to pass eight hours standing as punishment. Other prisoners, off and on, passed urine on the wall, but the political prisoners were not allowed to do this also.

Reading or exchanging books was considered an offence Barie maintained a thoroughly foolish point of view as far as reading of books was concerned. He would often say, "Non-sense. Shut up. I do not want to give these books of Kant or Vant. These people become assassins on reading such books. And all these books about *Yoga* or *Voga*, or theosophy are useless. But Superintendent (of jail) does not listen to me. I'm helpless and don't know what to do. I haven't read any book till today. Yet see, I'm a responsible person. Reading books is the job of women."

Once a political prisoner was reading the book on Geology. He took some notes from it in his notebook. Barie saw him doing this. He shouted, "I've caught you. What are you writing this secretly?" He asked Savarkar also regarding this. He told Barie that the prisoner was reading Geology. But Barie could not make any sense out of it. Since he was an Irish man, he did not follow English properly. Next day, as a punishment, that book was taken away from the prisoner for two weeks.

## Sacrifices of Political Prisoners

Some revolutionaries of Bengal had an encounter with police. Jyotish Chandra Pal, one young man among these revolutionaries, was wounded and caught. He was sentenced for life, and sent to Andamans. Here he was given his evening food and ordered to be put in his cell. When the constable was going to close the door, he asked him to get the toilet pan to be removed from there before he took his meals. The constable was not doing this. Jyotish Chandra Pal stuck to his words. The constable forcibly pushed him in, closed and locked the cell door and went away. The toilet pan remained there towards his head in the sleeping position for the whole night. He threw the food and started fasting. In a few days, he developed blood dysentery. He was admitted to the hospital. Veer Savarkar and all other political prisoners advised him to give up fasting, but he did not agree. In the end, horrible, mental tortures made him mad. He was kept in the mental asylum for a few days, and then sent back to Bengal. But this did not prove beneficial to him. One day people read the news of his tragic death in the papers.

Ram Rakkha was a Punjabi *Brahmin* who was arrested for propagating revolution in Burma and Siam, and deported to Andamans for life sentence. Here the *janeus* of prisoners were removed. Ram Rakkha had travelled to China, Japan etc., but he did not come across this kind of interference in religious matters of prisoners. He resisted the removal of his *janeu*. They tried to remove that forcibly, but he did not let that happen. So, his *janeu* was broken. He took a vow not to take food and water till a fresh *janeu* was made available to him. For fifteen days he did not take anything, and his condition grew serious. So a tube was put in through his rose, and he was force-fed. He did not budge from his stand, though this practice continued for fifteen days. He developed serious pain in his chest. The examination by the doctor revealed that he had developed tuberculosis. All the political prisoners got worried on knowing this. All of them requested him to give up his fast, but he did not agree. In the end Veer Savarkar persuaded him successfully to give up his fasting. But this did not help him. His condition maintained its downward slide, and in the end, he passed away, leaving much sadness behind him. The news somehow reached Indian newspapers. They raised their voice in this regard. So, the government was forced to frame a rule that in Andamans, religious symbols such as *janeu* will not be removed from prisoners.

**The Beating of Barie**

The conduct of the Pathan warders of jail with the prisoners was uncivilised. Once some new political prisoners were brought to this jail. These prisoners strongly protested the uncivilised behaviour of these worders. The matter reached Barie. Among these prisoners was a fearless youth named Parmanand. He was a resident of Jhansi. The jailor called him to his office. He saw this youth talking to somebody. He abused him, as per his habit. The young Parmanand could not bear this. He freed himself from warders, and gave two hard slaps on Barie's face. Barie ran out saying, "Get him, catch him." Parmanand was beaten mercilessly after this. He was bleeding all over. After beating, his wounds were dressed, and he was locked shut in the same cell.

After the beating of Barie, the terror of political prisoners spread to the whole Andamans. Since Barie had abused Parmanand, some political prisoners started a strike in protest. Now Barie and other supervisors came to their senses. They began advising and reasoning with the prisoners. The supervisors advised Barie not to abuse the prisoners. The prisoners were also told to do only that much of work as was possible with them. After this incident, the political prisoners were never rebuked to do more work.

No doubt, Parmanand brought the tortures of the political prisoners to an end by beating Barie. Though in return of this beating he was beaten much more, but the achievement of beating Barie was sufficient to forget all the pain that Parmanand suffered.

Pathan warders of jail behaved with Hindu prisoners in a beastly manner. So Veer Savarkar advised Hindu prisoners to organise themselves and face them. One day a Pathan warder, abusing a Tamil Hindu said, "This bloody fellow is a *Kafir.* The tuft-knot of hair on his head should be pulled and uprooted." Saying so, he laid his hands on the Hindu prisoner's tuft-knot of hair. That prisoner could not bear that misconduct. He pounced upon the warder, threw him upon the ground and sat on his chest, and started beating him with punches. The warder was frightened and said, "Please, excuse me." The Tamil prisoner did not know Hindi. He thought that the warder was abusing him and his mother. He became all the more furious. He beat the warder black and blue and rendered him unconscious. On this Veer Savarkar intervened and saved the warder, otherwise, he could have been killed. After this, Savarkar congratulated that prisoner for his courageous action.

**Exposure of Tortures in Jail**

Unbearable atrocities were perpetrated on political prisoners in jail, but the public in India was completely ignorant about it. So, it was thought that the public and the government of India should be apprised of it. But this work was not only difficult, it was well neigh impossible. This impossible work was rendered possible by Shri Hoti Lal Verma. Shri Verma was the ex-editor of *Swarajya*, a revolutionary paper. One of his editorials was treated as 'treasonous' by the government. As a result, he was sentenced to 10 years of imprisonment and sent to Andamans. He somehow arranged writing papers, and wrote a letter, describing the atrocities in jail. He was under the most strict watch and guard. Even then he succeeded in sending this letter out of jail.

This letter was delivered to Shri Surendra Nath, by some government officer who had sympathies with political prisoners. Surendra Babu published this letter in his newspaper. Along with this, discharging his duties as a fearless editor, he wrote an editorial also on this subject. Later on, many other newspapers also published this letter.

The prisoners were completely ignorant about the publication of this letter. One day, Barie himself revealed this secret to the prisoners in one of his bouts of foolishness. Describing this incident, Veer Savarkar wrote:

"One day the news of that letter reaching India was divulged by Barie himself unconsciously. It was early morning, and Barie was beside himself with rage. He abused right and left and insulted anybody whom he encountered. He struck his black stick on the ground hard as he walked pattering and blurting. We could not follow what the issue was. Barie was going round and shouting and admonishing the warders, saying, "You damned fellows, how do you manage? You'll ruin me."

A poisonous centipede is found in Andamans. If it bites, man cries with pain. On seeing Barie in this state of affairs, the prisoners whispered among themselves, "Possibly he is bitten by the centipede." Then Barie went towards Hoti Lal Verma, and for no rhyme or reason, started yelling loudly, "Keep standing! Why don't you hurry up! You are a big liar." Other persons could not understand the reason of this peculiar behaviour of Barie, but Hoti Lal knew that the letter must have been published. Barie was unusually angry. He did not know what he was blurting out. Then he started saying, "if you find a prisoner as close as ten steps to another prisoner, then correct it immediately. Political prisoners will now sit pretty apart for their meals. If somebody is seen going towards the prisoners, he will be punished."

Then taking the cover of a white lie, he started saying, "No one has so far committed a foolishness of this kind as done by one who sent this letter. You know what came out of it. As soon as the letter was published, a case was slapped on the newspaper. The press has been seized. Hoti Lal sent out a small letter due to his foolishness, but it caused a loss of two or three lakh rupees to the press owner and here the prisoners would face more strictness. Hoti Lal's sentence will be extended for writing a letter full of lies. In fact, he has done a base deed."

The secret behind this white lie of Barie soon bared itself. Slowly and slowly his arrogance changed into artificial politeness. Two weeks later, he said to Hoti Lal, "What can we do? Whatever is done is as per orders of the Government of India."

After this he said to Veer Savarkar, "Savarkar, see. This mad Hoti Babu of yours has strangulated a Bengali newspaper. The whole press has been seized."

Veer Savarkar spoke fearlessly, "But I fail to understand why this is happening. It seems the news is wrong. And if it is true, then, in an attempt to eliminate the sufferings of the political prisoners, we would not mind that many, and not one, presses are seized."

**Solitary Confinement**

Veer Savarkar and his elder brother Ganesh Savarkar were segregated from other prisoners because they demanded improvement in the food of prisoners. Even then, a few days later, the prisoners started hunger strike in support of this demand. The jail authorities attributed this strike to Savarkar brothers. So both the brothers were punished with solitary confinement. Thirteen months' solitary confinement, too, could not deflect them in any way. Solitary confinement was considered the most severe. A prisoner, in this confinement, developed a state of mind like that of a mad man.

Veer Savarkar had developed a language of signs for communication with other prisoners, and made other prisoners understand it beforehand. A chain was clanked with another chain to pass on different kinds of secret messages. During solitary confinement when Savarkar brothers were not allowed to see anybody, they communicated with and discussed things with fellow prisoners with the help of sound signs.

**Prisoners and Newspapers**

In Andamans, the prisoners were not allowed to have any kind of news about India. It has become almost impossible for them even to see the word 'Hindustan' printed on a piece of paper. If they found such a piece of papers, the prisoners swooped upon it. Once a piece of a newspaper was floating in a dirty drain. A lecture of Shri Gokhale was published in it, which expressed his disappointment over the education policy of the government. The prisoners look it out with the help of straws, and then spread it, again with the help of straws. Then everybody read it with great interest.

Elaborating on the helplessness of prisoners, Savarkar wrote:

"All the political prisoners were eager to know even the smallest, most insignificant news about India—whether a new factory was opened in India or one closed; a case started, or a riot took place; some new explosion of revolutionary activities or the rise of a new poet; i.e. any news, big or small, which gave indication of nature or progress of the long separated motherland. O India! These young men snatched from your lap are for ever worried about you. They forgot their physical pains. Revolutionary political prisoners, lodged in Andamans, were constantly keeping a tap on the nerve of their motherland, and through it estimated the health of their country, and undergoing happiness and agony, were passing their days...."

**Brothers Meet**

Veer Savarkar and his elder brother Ganesh Savarkar lived in the same jail for many years, but they were kept apart right from the very beginning. So, both the brothers could not even see each other. Veer Savarkar knew his elder brother's punishment and sentence in London itself, but the elder brother did not know anything about his younger brother. Both the brothers had never met ever sine the younger brother left for London. Veer Vinayak Savarkar harboured a strong desire to see his elder brother. He had requested the warders for their meeting, but due to the terror of Barie, no warder dared to help/oblige him. One day, in the evening, after getting the expelled oil measured, Veer Savarkar was returning to his cell, he met his elder brother by chance. Involuntarily, the words escaped from elder brother's mouth, "Tatya! You!!"

Tatya (Veer Savarkar) stopped, and wanted to talk to his elder brother, but the warders did not let them talk. Helpless, both the brothers headed towards their individual cells.

Next day, Veer Savarkar received a letter of his elder brother through the warder. It was written in the letter:

"Dear Tatya!

I hoped that you, though living abroad, would work for the freedom of the motherland. I suffered the deportation and sentence on the basis of that hope. My heart took these difficulties as insignificant. Both of us, brothers were locked in jails, and you alone, being out, were busy in the service of the motherland: this thought consoled me. It made the pains worth bearing. But how did you fall into their hands, while working in Paris. Now who will keep that flame of revolution burning? And 'Bal', our 'Bal', whom will he look up to? I have seen you myself, still I find it difficult to believe. Oh! My! How did you come here...?"

On reading this letter, he felt unusually mentally sad on realising failure in his duties. He too, sent a letter to his elder brother through the warder. Its main extracts are as follows:

"T , continue to struggle, after smearing one's body with the ashes of the physical and the rise of good fortune, this is divine good luck. Then why pain and suffering? Had I proved unsuccessful in test, my ability and duty would have been mired in dust. "सीदन्ति मम गात्राणि मुखं च परि शुष्यति। गांडीवं स्रंसते हस्तात् त्वक चैव परिदह्यते।" (*Sidanti mam gatrani mukham cha parishushyati, Gandivam sransate hastat tvak chaiva paridahyate*) (All parts of my body are getting numb, my mouth is drying, Gandiv is slipping out of my hands and my skin is burning). If I had deserted my post in this situation, whom would I show my face? But nothing like that has happened to me. On the other hand I have proved myself equal to the sufferings that came my way. Would I not have been dubbed as the deserter of duties if I ran away from the pains out of fear, which I exhorted Indian public to bear? In fact, the test of the sense of duty and ability of all of us is in bearing this suffering and pain. Glory or ignominy are just a matter of good or bad conjunction of events. See, Napolean passes away lying on an ordinary mat, though he was fighting all through life, had crossed the Lodi bridge and was victorious in Austrilitz. In the same way, fighting for freedom, warrior woman Lakshmi Bai's life is cut short by one blow of sword. Some soldiers die, wounded by the first blow. Their duty is not determined generally by good or bad co-incidences. I stay back in the battle, keep hidden and keep myself alive, whereas others are in forefront, winning and dying in the process of fighting. Shall I keep myself at the back and alive to enjoy the spoils of that fighting and winning? The real competence and sense of duty of a soldier depends on whether he harboured a cowardly, mischievous feeling running counter to public interest or not, or when the call of duty came, he fought or not in the forefront of battle with a dispassionate feeling. I understand each one of us has proved successful in that test. The aim of our life is to face difficulties, rot in prisons, and to die of the curse of those for whom we bore all this suffering. It is as great as to grapple to the tune of bugles or to strive for success and glory from outside. The reason is that to suffer in the caves, to moan in the prison houses and to lay down one's life unknowingly and hidden is as important as to visibly grapple with the problems for final victory and be stirred by the tunes of bugles."

On receiving this letter, Ganesh Savarkar experienced a sense of glory knowing the highest level of patriotism in his brother. He felt a divine satisfaction. Seeing the indomitable spirit of his brother, he forgot his sufferings.

**Purification in Jail**

Muslim warders of the jail frightened and terrorised Hindu youth prisoners to the extent that they were frustrated with their lives and contemplated suicide. After terrorising them in this manner, they showed pity and sympathy so as to coax them into accepting Islam. Veer Savarkar wrote:

"In Andamans, the three sinning, mischievous and liar warders posted to supervise Hindu political prisoners were all Pathan, Baluch and Punjabi Muslims. All the three cruel warders followed the policy of subjugating Hindus through terror. They had learnt a lesson in their childhood that torturing a Hindu was an act of redeeming all sins. Therefore, these mischievous warders caused different varieties of pain and torture to Hindu political prisoners. Irish Barie always sided with these sinful Muslims. Therefore all Sindhi Muslims, Pathan Muslims, Punjabi Muslims joined together in torturing Hindus."

Veer Savarkar saw that due to their cunningness one or two Hindus had accepted Islam. Therefore, they decided to effect purification as a retaliatory measure. The anger of these warders crossed all limits when they saw this. They threatened Savarkar to kill him, but in the face of Savarkar's determination they could not cause any harm to him.

Thus Veer Savarkar started the work of reconverting to Hinduism after purification of those Hindu youths who were forcibly converted to Islam. One day these warders had persuaded and prepared an Ahir youth, named Mullu, to accept Islam. Savarkar came to know of it. So, he decided to stop it. He contacted and descussed the matter with Sikh prisoners and reminded them the sacrifices made by the Sikh *gurus* for the protection of Hindu religion. The Sikh prisoners agreed to stop this religious conversion.

Muslims had made all preparations. All Muslim prisoners gathered at the place of this religious conversion. When Mullu Ahir was going to be administered the reading of *kalma*, Savarkar reached there with Sikh prisoners. All of them forcibly picked him (Mullu Ahir) up from there and left. Thus a Hindu was saved from accepting another religion. Then Savarkar made him understand the greatness of Hindu religion. He developed deep faith in Hindu religion after that.

### Adult Education in Jail by Savarkar

Veer Savarkar directed a programme of adult education in this prison. By spreading knowledge among prisoners, he wanted to create a new awakening among them. He organised a Self Study Group in jail in Andamans in order to realise this objective. He imparted instructions to prisoners undergoing life sentences in Andamans, of literature, politics, history, philosophy and Hindu religion. Two great personalities, Shri Ashutosh Lahiri and Bhai Parmanand, assisted him in this work. Veer Savarkar emphasised not only the study of Indian history, but the history of the whole world.

When the first World War started, then there was a slight improvement in the conduct of authorities vis-a-vis prisoners. They were permitted to get books, so whenever they wrote a letter to their friends or acquaintances they nearly always insisted upon sending books. In a very short time, they arranged 25,000 books in Andaman jail. They called this study group Nalanda University.

The studies in this university were carried on when they were twining ropes. It was at this time that Ashutosh Lahiri read out from books and explained it to others. Thus the studies and twining of ropes went on simultaneously. Savarkar was the Vice-Chancellor of this university and Shri Lahiri was Reader.

Veer Savarkar advised the prisoners to read the biographies of brave Mazzini, Garibaldi, and Guru Govind Singh. Parmanand, as mentioned earlier (one who beat Barie), completed his education in this university. He considered himself a graduate of this university. After being educated here, he became a teacher later on. He has recorded an incident during his student period here, in the following words:

"Once they gave me for reading a book, *Reich of Dutch Republic*. I tried my best efforts, but could not understand the real meaning of it. I told them about my weakness. On this they said, "Oh! There he was, one who wrote this beautiful book. And here you are, one who is not following this book. Will you fight the British power with this intelligence and little knowledge? Read, read again." They told me the qualities of studies. 'Take one sleep in the night and get up. That is the right time for reading and writing. Our *Rishis* and *Munis* carried on with their studies and *sadhna* at this time. They meditated. This is called *Brahma-Akash Muhurta*. There is peace all around. Total silence. At that time the sky becomes endless. Mother earth comes and stands before you in the guise of Nature, enveloping all the mysteries of the Endless."

## Writing Poems in the Prison

The rigours of Andaman prison could not silence the poetic heart of Veer Savarkar. Though he was harnessed as a bullock in the expeller, he did not turn his eyes away from poetry. He had a strong desire in heart to write an epic poem. So he became busy in the creation of an epic poem. Ignoring the physical and mental suffering of this place, the poems he has written are not only appreciable but admirable and respectable as well.

It was during this time that great poet Rabindra Nath was awarded the Nobel Prize. He became a world poet. Veer Savarkar got this news in the Andaman jail. An Indian got this prestigious award, so Veer Savarkar considered it a matter of pride for Indians. He wrote a poem on this occasion to congratulate the great poet Tagore. In Andaman jail he wrote three great poems, '*Kamla, Gomantak* and *Virahochchhavas*'. There was practically no writing material available in jail. By writing these poems Veer Savarkar made possible what was impossible. Exemplifying the saying 'where there is a will, there is a way', he wrote his poems by scratching them on the wall of his cell by coal or stone and then remembered them by heart.

## Statues and Ganga—Symbols of Cultural Faith

India, Indian culture, its liberal traditions or every speck of dust of India—everything was equivalent to a God of Worship for Veer Savarkar. He considered every temple, place of religious pilgrimage or river a cultural heritage of India. Pandit Parmanand of Jhansi was under the influence of thinking of progressive Arya Samaj. One day he expressed his ideas opposing idol worship before Veer Savarkar. Then Savarkar, reflecting on his objectives, asked him, "Parmanand Ji! Have you ever had a *darshan* of Lord Veshwanath in Kashi?"

"No, I don't believe in idol worship", replied Pandit Parmanand.

On this, with great affection, Veer Savarkar said, "Parmanand Ji! Don't you know that Kashi is lakhs of years old city? It is a symbol of ancient Indian culture, civilisation and history. This idol of Vishwanath in Kashi is thousands of years old, ancient. For thousands of years Hindus have made great sacrifices for the protection of their status and temples on the basis of their faith, renunciation and *tapasya*. For thousands of years, the Hindu community has kept its *shraddha*, faith, commitment and feelings of love for its country and religion ablaze in the worship of these historical idols... Is that idol an ordinary stone today, which has been coronated for thousands of years by Shivaji, *Maharana* Pratap, *Maharani* Ahalya Bai, Nana Saheb, and many other brave persons such as Chhatrasal with their blood, and which has been worshipped with heart, adorations and *mantras* by countless people?"

"Mother Ganga is such an invaluable heritage of our India where the bones—flowers of great men from *satyug* to *Kalyug* are stored and preserved. The moment you take a bath there- in, a living feeling for our religion and nation surges in the heart sitting on its banks the *Vedic Rishis* declared the Hindu culture to the world. It declares and nurtures the emotional unity of the whole country, our Ganga *Mata*."

Pandit Parmanand was highly impressed by this lecture.

**Revolutionary Letters**

When you are far away from your family and acquaintances, then the medium of communication and information which is most convenient is the writing of letters. When Veer Savarkar was far away from his motherland, and was leading the life of an exiled person as a prisoner in Andamans, he wrote letters to his respected sister-in-law, and other acquaintances. He was permitted to write just one letter in a year, during his imprisonment. Even then these are not ordinary letters. They are the letters full of his spirit eager to sacrifice everything for his motherland. Some extracts from some of his important letters are given below:

"Dear Bal!

You must be observing that our generation is born at such a time and in such a country where it has become obligatory that every kind and honest hearted person chooses for himself a path which passes through sighs and separations. This path is the path of duty and action. A heart which has turned into a hard stone, one that has experienced the cruel blows of cycles of destiny, one that understands the daily routine of creation of tortures and disappointments—it seems that this order is fixed at least for me in the scheme of nature. Therefore, when happiness comes my way, then this heart sees it all the more as to how transitory and impermanent is this good gesture, and to what extent it is good in comparison to state of things at my end. I have always treated tears as a source of happiness. Whatever be the case, time is changing, and with the change of fortune, friends are returning to me... One day when we, my elder brother and I, met for some time, I said to elder brother, "*Shastras* mention *dev-rina, pitra-rina* and *rishi-rina*. Likewise there is a *putra-rina* also in the world. On reading your letter I felt that I am completely free from that debt, because now you are thoroughly educated and endowed with the strength useful for the world... Madama Cama has consistently maintained her affection for us. Even war has not succeeded in diverting her attention from you. Sometimes selected persons are more useful than relatives. There is an affection in the world, which can be comprehended only by the best heart, and which cannot be snapped even by a blood relation or special benefit. It is born in an ideal soil, and it is nourished by those subtle powers which the worldly people can neither see nor comprehend."

"Dear friend!

The resolution of the Andhra Parishad was drafted in a definite and comprehensive form, which showed that the residents of Andhra Pradesh had full and sincere sympathy. Those people made an effort to free mother India, with their good or bad means but with total dedication and sincerity and completely renouncing selfishness, and for that reason alone they are rotting and dying in jails. You have written that many newspapers are trying (through continuous writing) to get the political prisoners freed, and hope that the disturbances in the country may slightly come down in this manner. If this is all right, then I fail to understand why the Congress party is still hesitating. Why is it afraid of saying a single word, which does not show sympathy, but just oozes out a smell of humanity. Sympathy, for what?

For the political prisoners of those people, whose representative the Congress claims to be. Last year the Congress passed a resolution for the release of persons placed under house arrest in different provinces... whose work and sacrifice is in no way less than our brothers under house arrest, and whose sufferings will not automatically cease with the ending of War, as would be in the case of persons under house arrest. Therefore, those people, who are called responsible leaders of the people, should carry on a more vigorous agitation... we will find unbearable to live in that country where every person traversing the path of progress will be punished. It is written that it is difficult to walk on a path where every step is a step in a doubtful direction, where every step ahead invites the wrath of the *sultan* sitting ahead, and where every step backward angers a man's self-respect and wisdom, which are no less than a *sultan* at their places. Anger, threats and sighs, and the foul smell which renders the heart restless and weak, have tried to block the best breath of my life, but God has given me strength to bear and bear with fortitude, and I have faced it all for the last eight years. I have a feeling that my body has suffered a wound which does not tend to heal, and because of which my body is slowly and slowly wasting itself.

But all these things apply only to body, to flesh. If a man is compelled to live on a pile of burning flames, he cannot be free form the fear of those flames. Even then my spirit today can rule my trembling body. Even today it is ready to bear more hardships happily, without taking a step back. Brother's health is better than mine, though due to headache his weight is reduced to 106 pounds.

Your brother Tatya.

(V.D. Savarkar)"

"Dear Bal and Shrimati Shanta!

Elder brother and I congratulate you on the occasion of your entering into the married life, the second stage of life.

You have fully discharged the duties and responsibilities of the first stage of life. When a storm was brewing on our motherland, you stood your fixed ground, firmly and dispassionately. Storm came and beat, but you stood fearlessly and honestly. You continued to remain sincere and honest, though surrounded by many traitors. You have demonstrated that enthusiasm and confidence, to inculcate which among its youngmen Europe has devised honours like Aryan Cross and Victoria Cross. You gave up the prize of appreciation from the public. Therefore, I say that you have completed the first stage of your life in the full and best manner. Dear Bal! And Shanta! Now you are entering into a happy and better stage of life, that of conjugal life. Dear Bal! May God cover your path with roses, and Dear Shanta! May God develop your youth into immortal gold. May the cluster of your thoughts be happy and flowered in the happiness of the heaven of conjugal life, a heaven that has survived the destruction of heaven. May the early sunrise, the evening and every particle of the earth be sweet and loving for you!

In the end, the expected has nearly happened. I desire to see those times when inter-province marriages will take place among Hindus and all the walls of caste and religion crumble down to earth. The vast river of our Hindu life, crossing through all the marshes and deserts, will flow pious and strong. Its flow will not face any obstacles, nor will there be any possibility of blocks in future. However, the foremost thing to be done in this regard is to accord hight place and right to love in married life and relations. We should not close our eyes to the fact that though we are paying special attention at present towards improving the breed of animals and birds, we are not paying similar attention for better breeding of men. For hundreds of years we have married small children, and that, too, through the middle men. For hundreds of years, love has been displaced from his effective seat. Therefore, those elements are not developing through which body, soul and mind improve. This has invariably resulted into our short and weak bread whose life-strength and manly power is destroyed. Our system of marriage is also a main reason among thousand others for this consequence. People should come forward to make love holy and pious, and not to stop it...You have written that there is a stir in your world due to world war. But it has not even touched me nor my Port Blair. This little state of ours can proudly state in its annual speech that our interests or vulnerable points have remained completely untouched by this worldwide storm. There was no change in our import or export... He will live only when man has banished war. Otherwise, we will just exist, with so much of strength and fixity that even the world of death will feel ashamed... Don't worry for me that I live in darkness, and that when other men and women are focussing light according to their intelligence on the direction of mankind then I am just waiting here. Do you not remember the sentiments in the famous poet Milton's poem, "His kingdom is mighty. Thousands at His bidding speed... They also serve who sit and wait." And whom do they serve; they not only wait, they suffer as well and still are on their post of duty. One who works is better because he places one stone atop another. He chisels it. But isn't the lime and mortar of God's temple important? It is this who suffers. It is the mortar bathed in blood.

Affectionately Yours

Tatya

(V.D. Savarkar)"

**Return from Andamans**

The British government thought that deportation to Andamans would break Veer Savarkar and he would give up his revolutionary thoughts. But nothing of this sort happened. The lion, though caged, is still a lion. He was subjected to horrible physical and mental tortures in the death cell of Andamans, which totally destroyed his health. Seeing his condition, the doctors seriously apprehended that it might convert into chronic T.B. He was taking only milk for one full year. Famous revolutionary Bhai Parmanand was also in this jail during this time. When he was freed in 1920 and returned to India, he got busy in efforts to get Veer Savarkar freed. The British M.P. Karl Wedgewood came to India during this period. He was a friend of Lala Lajpat Rai, so when he came to Lahore he was a guest of Lalaji. Courtesy Lalaji, Bhai Parmanand met Wedgewood. He talked to Wedgewood regarding setting Veer Savarkar free. Wedgewood promised to take up the matter and make serious efforts. When he has returning to England, he met the governor of Bombay province and requested him for the release of Savarkar. The governor informed him that his tenure was shortly going to be completed and another governor was coming to take the charge over from him. So Wedgewood in London met the new governor and made a similar request to him. The governor accepted his request, and so on assuming his charge after coming to Bombay, he ordered the release of Savarkar brothers on health grounds.

On 21st January, 1921 Veer Savarkar's D-Card (symbol of his being dangerous) was removed. He was surprised on it, but he did not know that he was returning to India. A few days later, a warder gave him a letter, indicating, "Now you will be kept in Bombay jail." In the happiness of seeing his motherland again, he started preparing for his return.

On 10th February, 1921 Veer Savarkar and his elder brother Ganesh Savarkar left for their motherland. When he was leaving the prison, other inmates garlanded him and offered their good wishes. Both the brothers left for India in a ship named, *Maharaja*. Due to lack of space in the ship, they were first lodged in the cabins meant for mad persons. Later on the cabins were exchanged, but both the brothers were not kept in one cabin. On the 4th day after leaving Andamans, both the brothers reached their motherland, India.

# Confinement in Ratnagiri

Veer Savarkar, on reaching India from Andamans, was lodged in Alirajpur jail of Calcutta. Nearly three years after his stay in this jail, he was sent to Ratnagiri in January, 1924.

Ratnagiri was a small village only at that time. From 6th January, 1924 he was put under house arrest here. When he was sent from Calcutta it was stated that his house arrest was for a period of 5 years, but on the expiry of this period, the government increased his house arrest for an indefinite period, stating that his activities were harmful for the government. Of course, he was granted some limited freedom. He was free to move in the district, and people could contact him. He made the best use of this limited freedom. He organised *Hindu Mahasabha* and did not let go from his hands any opportunity of spreading religion and culture. He wrote a few books also during this period, namely *Hindutva, Hindupad Padshahi, Shaap, Uttar-kriya* etc. Besides, he directly or indirectly directed important historic activities such as *Shuddhi Andolan* during this period.

**Contribution to Purification Activities**

During his confinement to Ratnagiri, Veer Savarkar saw, heard and experienced that in India, and the Portugese ruled Goa, Hindus were being converted to other religions forcibly, fraudulently, or through some incentives. By establishing *Hindu Mahasabha* in Ratnagiri, he successfully, and with great zeal, carried on *Shuddhi Andolan* for thirteen years.

Thousands of Hindus in Goa were converted to Christianity in this manner. There a *Mahatma,* named Vinayak Maharaj Masoorkar, was directing the *shuddhi* of religionwise converted Hindus. This man in his student life was a member of the forum *'Abhinav Bharat'* of Veer Savarkar, and his original name was Shri Vinayak Joshi. His elder brother, in the guise of an astrologer, was observing the conditions in Goa secretly, along with his disciples. In 1928, Swami Masoorkar purified 10,000 persons and reconverted them to Hinduism. This, as a consequence, created a stir among Christians there. Swami Masoorkar and his disciples were arrested by the Goa government. Veer Savarkar received this news in Ratnagiri. He felt very sad. The very next day he collected eight hundred rupees and remitted them for the help of Swamiji and asked Dr. Munje and Shri Kelkar, leaders of Hindu Mahasabha, to go to Goa and talk to the government there. Questions were raised in Bombay Assembly, Central Assembly of India, and in the British and Portugese Parliaments regarding the arrest of Swami Masoorkar. In the end Swami Masoorkar and his disciples were released. It was due to efforts of Swami Masoorkar that Goa was a Hindu majority island and finally merged in the Indian Union.

Sometime after Veer Savarkar's arrival in Ratnagiri, the whole district was in the grip of severe plague. Resultingly, he was sent to Nasik. The *Mahars* of Nasik were preparing for conversion to *Aghakhani* Muslims. They were saved from this conversion due to the efforts of Savarkar. He carried on similar activities in Ratnagiri also. Here *dheevars, bhandaris*, and other Hindus of *Vaishyavani* caste carried on overseas trade. During the period of Chhatrapati Shivaji, their ancestors worked in fleets of boats. At this time *dheevars* were slowly and slowly converting to Islam. Veer Savarkar reminded them the great traditions of their ancestors, and re-converted *dheevars* to Hinduism through his *shuddhi andolan*.

Near about 1926, Tukoji Rao Holkar, the ruler of Indore wanted to marry Miss Miller, a Christian maid, but the orthodox Hindu society was opposing this. Veer Savarkar wrote a letter to *Maharaj* Holkar that he (Savarkar) would fully support him in this activity. If a *pundit* was not ready and available for Miss Miller's *shuddhi* and her marriage, he would arrange and despatch a *pundit*.

Many young girls of other religions were initiated into

Hindu religion in Ratnagiri. Taking inspiration from Veer Savarkar many Hindu youths married those maids. Generally, the parents of the bride, or groom, or of both did not turn up in such marriages. Savarkar took upon himself that role on these occasions.

Christian missionaries opposed tooth and nail the *shuddhi andolan* of Veer Savarkar. They sent many letters to the governor of Bombay opposing this. The British government also became unhappy with this activity of Savarkar. As a result, the government asked an explanation from him. On this he wrote to the government in clear words, "Since there is freedom of religious conversion under your rule, then the *shuddhi* activity of the Hindus cannot be prohibited. First stop the conversion of Hindus to Christianity, after that a thought would be given to the stoppage of *shuddhi* activity."

Besides Christians, Muslims, too, were highly irritated at *shuddhi karan.* Not only this. Even orthodox Hindus also opposed it. But Veer Savarkar did not care for it. He carried on this movement all through his life. In his will be clearly mentioned that after his death five thousand rupees, out of his share of money, should be spent on *shuddhi* activities.

**Removal of Untouchability**

Untouchability is a blot on Hindu society, which has disintegrated it for centuries. Veer Savarkar was a true *Brahmin.* A true *Brahmin* can never support such wrong traditions. Therefore, he made untiring efforts to remove this blot on Hindu society. Veer Savarkar organised community lunches and dinners for *savarnas* (upper caste Hindus) and *asavarnas* (low caste) to forge unity among them. Swami Samatanand (original name Anant Hari Garde), one of his disciples, rendered him appreciable co-operation in this work. Swami Samatanand got the work of *Satyanarayan* worship performed by people considered to be untouchables. After the worship, they distributed the *prasad* of God and *savarna* women applied *tilak* to their foreheads. He organised these activities on a large scale in Maharashtra. Off and on orthodox *savarna* Hindus opposed this activity, but the reformer of Hindu society Veer Savarkar did not pay any heed to them or cared for it.

Gandhiji had sympathies for *Harijans*. Dr. Bhim Rao Ambedkar, too, started an agitation for the uplift of *dalits* (downtrodden). His objective was to help them attain a respectable life, by obtaining social and political rights for them. He advised *Harijans* to give up Hindu religion, and under his own leadership many Harijans, renouncing Hindu religion, were initiated into Buddhism. The point of view of Veer Savarkar was totally different from that of Gandhiji and Ambedkar. He did not consider sympathy towards, or religious conversion by *Harijans* a solution of the problem of untouchability. He did not consider only sympathy or class struggle proper in this regard. He bitterly criticised the proposal for religious conversion of *Harijans* by Dr. Bhim Rao. He favoured bringing in equity in Hindu society through reform in all its classes. He wanted Hindu religion to be rid of orthodoxies, and grow into a scientific religion. He started movements from time to time to give concrete shape to his ideas in this regard.

*Harijan* children were not admitted to primary schools in the society those days. Resultingly, these children went to Christian missionary schools for education, where the missionaries very conveniently turned them away from Hinduism and converted them to Christianity. Veer Savarkar started a movement to get *Harijan* children admitted to the schools for *savarna* children. He was successful in his efforts and *Harijan* children started studying with *savarna* children.

Maulana Mohammed Ali, president of the Koknada session of the Congress Party, while delivering his presidential address, proposed that *Harijans* should be divided equally among Hindus and Muslims. It is said he got this idea from Aga Khan, the leader of Muslim League. Gandhiji, too, could not oppose this proposal of the *Maulana*. Veer Savarkar, expressing his strong reaction to this statement, said:

"Mohammed Ali, who wanted to gobble seven crore untouchable brothers with the help of *Congressi* Hindus, and Gandhiji, who out of his innocence supported him, cannot be the friends of Hindu society."

It was the opinion of Veer Savarkar that *Acharyas* and *Mahatmas* of Hindu religion should also contribute towards eradication of untouchability from Hindu society. When he was in Ratnagiri, once *Jagadguru* Shankaracharya had also visited that place. On advice and permission from Veer Savarkar, he accepted garlands from persons of *Mahar* and *sweeper* community of Hindus.

It is apparent from all these facts that Veer Savarkar was a real and sincere well-wisher of *asavarnas* and Hindu society. He considered *asavarnas* as an inalienable part of Hindu society, and wanted to give them a respectable place in society equal to that of *savarnas*.

**Meeting Important Persons**

When Savarkar was under house arrest in Ratnagiri, many leaders of national level, social reformers and others came to meet him, with whom he discussed the then politics, religion, culture and many other allied issues. In 1924 when due to spread of plague in Ratnagiri, Savarkar was taken to Nasik for some time, then Dr. Munje and *Jagadaguru* Shankaracharya welcomed him. This reception ceremony was held in Kale Ram Temple. Besides the above mentioned great personalities, many citizens also participated in it. The famous journalist and editor of *kesari*, Shri Narsimha Chintamani Kelkar, presented him with a welcome address. In reply to his reception, Veer Savarkar said, "How should I reply for the way you have honoured me... I was satisfied even when I lived in a death cell in Andamans. I thought that I would die there. Whatever I did, I did with a dispassionate heart, and therefore I did not feel any pain. This never occurred to me that I would be honoured in this manner. There would be many youngmen in the meeting today. On seeing me honoured, they should not presume that service to caste, religion or society is rendered for gaining honour.

"Young Men! See towards those people who were born for the spread and propagation of religion and who are called martyrs today. Jesus Christ looked towards the cross and not towards honour. When Shivaji *Maharaj* was taken captive, he never dreamt of any coronation. Die working for your religion. The moment you start your work, understand that you have to traverse a path of thorns.

"A young man of Sparta was wounded in a battle. When people asked him how he should be honoured as Sparta was victorious due to him, then that brave man said, 'Write on my tomb "Sparta has more able sons, and the coming generation will be still better." I also do that. A thousand times more brilliant and strong men than me are there in the country and in future there will be many more."

In 1925 Dr. Keshav Rao Balirao Hedgewar met Veer Savarkar in Shirgaon, Ratnagiri. He had not organised the *Rashtriya Swayam Sewak Sangh* by then. Dr. Hedgewar discussed with Veer Savarkar about forming some national organisation for Hindus. Savarkar was very happy with this idea of a national Hindu organisation and promised to extend his total support to Dr. Hedgewar in this work. Immediately after his release from Ratnagiri, on 12th December 1937 in Nagpur he expected of *Rashtriya Swayam Sewak Sangh* that it would impart training in the use of arms to Hindu youths, besides awakening them culturally. He participated in many programmes of *Sangh* after this.

In 1924 *Maulana* Mohammed Ali, the famous leader of the Congress, also met Veer Savarkar. He praised him liberally for his patriotism and the spirit of renunciation, but opposed his *shuddhi* movement. On this Savarkar told him categorically that first the *mullahs* and *maulvis* should be stopped from converting Hindus to Islam, and only after that some thought would be spared for stopping the *shuddhi* movement. Veer Savarkar expressed his ideas in opposition to the movement against the Congress Party also. On this *Maulana* Mohammed Ali became angry and he blurted out effortlessly, "If these suggestions of Mussalmans are not accepted, then there are many countries in the world, and Muslims would be compelled to go there."

Hearing such words coming from the lips of a leader of national stature, Savarkar said in the most clear terms, "You are absolutely free. Frontier Mail goes out of country every day. What are you waiting for? Pack up your bag and baggage and leave India immediately."

*Maulana* Mohammed Ali had not expected that he would get a reply of this sort. Getting irritated, he said, "You are too small for me. Therefore, I can pounce and crush you."

Veer Savarkar replied immediately, "I accept your challenge. Possibly you do not know Shivaji was also a dwarf before Afzal Khan, but this *Maratha* of low stature tore apart the belly of this huge *Pathan*." On hearing this the *Maulana* was made to realise his status.

Mahatma Gandhi also came to meet Veer Savarkar in Ratnagiri in March, 1927. Though there was a fundamental difference in the thinking of these two great men, Gandhiji was a great admirer of Savarkar's knowledge, patriotism, renunciation and other virtues. Gandhiji also started criticising his *shuddhi* movement. On this Veer Savarkar fearlessly put forth Gandhiji, "Muslims have forcibly converted Hindus to Islam, carrying *Quoran* in one hand and sword in the other. In this situation to make Hindus aware of the importance of their religion and to bring them back to it is a national work (duty)."

Along with this he cautioned Gandhi against the plan of leaders of Muslim League who wanted to convert India into a Muslim nation.

The revolutionary youths of India were highly influenced by Savarkar's *1857 ka Swatantrya Samar*. This book was called the *Geeta* of the revolutionaries. Bhagat Singh, noblest among martyrs, had secretly published it and made it available to the revolutionaries. He was highly impressed by Veer Savarkar. In 1928 he paid a secret visit to Ratnagiri and met Savarkar. In fact, he received Savarkar's permission to publish this voluminous book, in this meeting. Both the brave men held long and detailed discussions regarding the freedom of their motherland.

In addition to the above mentioned persons, many others including revolutionary martyr Sukh Dev, Vaishampayan, Basudev Balwant Gopate, the revolutionary behind Hudson *kand*, Dr. Ambedkar, Shri Achyut Patwardhan, *Senapati* Bapat, revolutionary V.S. Iyer, Nani Gopal, famous historian Govind Sakharam Sardesai, Dr. Kelkar, the famous compiler of Marathi Encyclopaedia, Marathi poet Dr. Patwardhan, Socialist leader Meher Yusuf Ali, Thakur Chandan Singh, the President of *Nepali Gorkha Sabha*, and others met Veer Savarkar and discussed issues with him.

Thakur Chandan Singh, the President of the *Nepali Gorkha Sabha*, came with a delegation. He was so impressed by the personality and ideas of Veer Savarkar that he compared him with Napoleon. After this meting he said, "Now I know what kind of impressive personality was the French Commander Napoleon."

**Purification Work of Hindi Language**

Though the mother tongue of Veer Savarkar was Marathi, he considered Hindi language and its *Dev-nagari* script an important medium of national unity. That is why during his prison life in Andamans he propagated Hindi and *Dev-nagari*. He carried on this movement during his house arrest in Ratnagiri also. For this he wrote an article, titled *Bhasha Shuddhi*. Through the medium of this article he supported a pure Sanskrit oriented Hindi and proposed a boycott of words of Urdu and English languages etc. He publicised his views in the newspapers to make *nagari* script standardised and fit for printing and typing. Later on he wrote a book, *Nagari Lipi Sudhar*, also on this subject. He was the first to bring into currency alphabets of Hindi (*Barahkhari*) (from अ to ज्ञ). His opinion in this regard was accepted by *Rashtra Bhasha Prachar Samiti*, Wardha also.

His views were very clear that if all the speakers of different languages in India start writing their languages in *nagari* scripti, then the language problem of India will be solved with ease. Well-known literature and political leader *Rajarshi* Purushottam Das Tandon was highly impressed by Savarkar's proposal of Sanskrit oriented Hindi. He said that the idea of Sanskrit oriented Hindi had come to him from Veer Savarkar. It was on Veer Savarkar's advice that his revolutionary friend Shri Ganesh Raghunath Vaishampayan founded *Hindi Pracharak Sabha* in Poona and started a movement in Maharashtra for the propagation of Hindi. Shri Vaishampayan translated into Hindi Savarkar's tome *1857 ka Swatantrya Samar*.

Gandhiji was a supporter of Urdu mixed '*Hindustani*.' He proposed that Lord Ram could be addressed as *Shehzada*

Ram, *Raja Dashrath* as *Badshah* Dashrath, *Mata* Sita as *Begum* Sita, *Maharshi* Valmiki as *Maulana* Valmiki etc. Savarkar was totally opposed to this proposal. '*Hindi Rashtra Bhasha Sammelan*' was organised in Poona with the efforts of Shri Vaishampayan. It was presided over by *Rajarshi* Tandon. Gandhiji's above proposal was rejected in this *Sammelan*.

Particularly worth noting is this fact also that Veer Savarkar coined many new words in Hindi. For instance the word '*Mahapaur*' for Mayor, '*Upmudrit*' for proof, '*Ekatva*' for monopoly etc. are the words discovered and coined by Veer Savarkar. He expressed his ideas of boycott of outside words through the medium of newspapers and in meetings and *sammelans* related to languages.

### A Weekly Paper in Memory of Swami Shraddhanand

In 1926 when Veer Savarkar was starting his *shuddhi* movement from Ratnagiri Swami Shraddhanand in North-India was carrying on a similar work, putting his heart and soul into it. On 23rd December, 1926 an assassin Abdul Rashid murdered Swamiji. This incident plunged the whole country into grief.

Veer Savarkar found similarity in his views with those of Swamiji on issues such as *shuddhi* movement, Hindu culture, patriotism etc. On Swamiji's assassination a condolence meeting was held in Ratnagiri also, as in other parts of the country, where Veer Savarkar gave a touching lecture. A few days after this in 1927 he called his younger brother Dr. Narayan Savarkar and advised him to bring out two papers. One of the papers was *Shraddhanand* which was in pious memory of Swami Shraddhanand. The name of the other paper was *Hutatma*. In the first issue of the weekly, *Shraddhanand*, was published an article entitled '*Shraddhanandji ki Hatya*', which was a topic of discussion for quite a few days then. Veer Savarkar continued to advise his brother off and on regarding the paper. His articles in this paper were published by some other name or in the name of Narayan Rao Savarkar.

**Freedom from Ratnagiri**

It has already been stated that initially Veer Savarkar was confined to Ratnagiri for five years. Subsequently this time was extended to an indefinite period.

In 1937 a new rule was framed in Parliament, under which the direction of provincial government was to be handed over to the representatives of the public, but their rights to carry on the functions of the government were limited. In accordance with this rule, elections were held all over the country. In these elections, the Congress got majority in seven states including Bombay, but it refused to form government. Therefore, the governors constituted temporary cabinets. Likewise in Bombay, Dhanji-Sha Kapoor, who was in minority, accepted the invitation to form government. He invited Shri Jamna Das Mehta, the leader of Lokshahi Swarajya Dal, to join his cabinet. Shri Mehta was a very close friend of Veer Savarkar. He put forth the condition of release of Veer Savarkar for joining the cabinet. Shri Kapoor accepted this condition. So on 10th May, 1937 when Shri Mehta became a minister, Veer Savarkar was released from Ratnagiri.

# Freedom and After

A wave of joy swept through the whole country on the release of Veer Savarkar. First of all, a very big meeting was held in Ratnagiri. When he went to Kolhapur, after this, a big meeting was held there as well. Meetings and congregations were organised at other places also though Veer Savarkar was not present there. Now Veer Savarkar started planning his future programmes.

**Tour of the Country**

After his release from house arrest in Ratnagiri, Veer Savarkar toured and visited many important places in different states of India between 1937 and 1943. First of all he visited Delhi in 1938, where a warm and grand reception was held in his honour. People distributed sweets and showered flowers on him.

Uttar Pradesh was the centre of the 1857 fight for freedom. On 3rd April, 1938, Veer Savarkar reached Kanpur. People welcomed him very warmly, expressing happiness on his arrival. In an assembly held in his honour, Veer Savarkar said, "It is the same Kanpur which saw the defeat of the British army. Here *Senapati* Tatya Tope defeated the Britishers. I had a very strong desire in my heart since childhood to visit Kanpur and Benaras. It is my good fortune that day is today. I have been hearing in dreams since my childhood the sound of slogans and artillery guns of the army of Nana Saheb and Tatya Tope. Today I am seeing that land with my own eyes."

After this he went to see the famous Ganga Ghat where the Englishmen were sacrificed. Then he visited Shiva Temple where, by blowing the conch, Tatya Tope had declared his battle. From Kanpur he went to Faizabad and Barabanki, and then returned to Lucknow. Here he met *Acharya* Narendra Dev. Then from Lucknow he went to Agra.

In April, 1938 he toured Solapur and on 10th May this year, he inaugurated *Hindu Yuvak Parishad* in Poona. His elder brother, Ganesh Savarkar, Dr. Hedgewar, Swami Masoorkar and others were present on this occasion. A few days later he went to Punjab. In Punjab first he went to Lahore and then visited the Golden Temple in Amritsar. Here a sword was presented to him in his honour. On his way to Bombay from there, he reached Ajmer, and from there to Jodhpur, and finally he reached Sindh via Nasik and Gwalior. He was accorded warm and huge receptions in Karachi, Hyderabad and Sakkhar cities of Sindh state.

In Sakkhar, from the platform of *Hindu Parishad*, he pointed towards a dark future for the Hindus of Sindh and its ill consequences for them on the formation of Pakistan, and advised them to oppose the Congress policy of appeasement. In March, 1939 he participated in *Bihar Hindu Parishad* and delivered an encouraging speech. In the first week of June he participated in the *sammelan* of *Mahakaushal Hindu Sabha*. Here the municipality of the area honoured him and presented a citation. In September he toured the villages and cities of Karnataka such as Dharwar, Hosur, Bel-Hongal and others. In October he reached Meerut where some anti-social elements attacked his procession. The government of United Provinces put a ban on his procession. Pandit Govind Vallabh Pant was the Chief Minister of United Provinces then.

In December, 1939 the annual session of *Akhil Bhartiya Hindu Mahasabha* was held in Calcutta. When Veer Savarkar reached there from Bombay, he was accorded a rousing and excited welcome. It was the biggest session of Hindu Mahasabha in history. Wherever Veer Savarkar went, a huge and surging crowd turned up for his reception. He could not sleep for two days. Scented rose water and flowers were showered on him. In this session he invited the king of Nepal for dinner, but Savarkar fell ill at the time of dinner party. Therefore, the king of Nepal himself went over to Veer Savarkar to enquire about his health. Both of them talked politics for about an hour. On this occasion, Shri N.R. Sarkar, a member of the Executive Council of Governor, also came to see him.

In March, 1940, Veer Savarkar toured different parts

and places in Karnataka. He presided over the session of *Karnataka Hindu Parishad.* From there he reached Madras. In one meeting here, he opposed the demand for Pakistan. Next day there was another in which there was a talk on Shivaji. From Madras he proceeded on a tour of Kerala. In Quilon he was the guest of the king of Travancore (Kerala). The Changanacherry Municipality honoured him with a citation. There the representatives of *Harijans* and Christians met him. Speaking in Changanacherry, he focussed light on the point of view of Hindu Mahasabha regarding its policy of Indian kings and rulers, and emphasised the need for *shuddhi* activities. He was welcomed in a grand style in Tinvelli, Kolipatti, Satur, Virudh Nagar and other places. In Madurai the *acharyas* of Meenakshi Temple welcomed him and took him out in a procession on a decorated elephant with saffron flag.

Savarkar's health began to deteriorate in the second half of 1940 due to his continuous travelling. Even then in the month of December he attended the session of *Akhil Bharatiya Hindu Mahasabha* and delivered presidential address. In January, 1941 he participated in the centenary celebrations of Nasik Library and Reading Room. In July, 1941 he was in Calcutta to lay with his own hands the foundation of Ashutosh Mukherjee Convention Hall. During this month itself a meeting was organised under the presidentship of Shri Saproo. Speaking in this meeting, Veer Savarkar gave the slogan of united India. After this he was welcomed in Sangli and a meeting was held opposing the idea of creation of Pakistan. Savarkar reached Assam in November, 1941. The public welcomed him in a grand style in Shillong. Muslims were entering Assam at that time in very large numbers. Veer Savarkar warned against the long-range dangerous consequences of this move. In reply to Savarkar, Nehru said in a speech, "There is a lot of unoccupied space in Assam. Native does not want that space should remain unoccupied." Opposing this, Veer Savarkar in his speech said, "Pandit Nehru is neither a philosopher nor an expert in classic scriptures. He does not know that Nature wants to remove poisonous air."

In December, 1942 Veer Savarkar was made the president of the Kanpur session of *Akhil Bharatiya Hindu Mahasabha.*

## Meeting the Viceroy

The World War II started in September, 1939. Lord Linlithgo, Viceroy invited with honour Veer Savarkar on 9th October, 1939 to meet him. The main purpose of the Viceroy was to know the thinking of Savarkar at this time. Veer Savarkar stated in very clear words, "I am a revolutionary, therefore, I support militarisation in the interest of the country. It is necessary to post Sikh and Gorkha platoons in the interest of Hindus. But, in reality, India is most likely to be attacked in the east." Lord Linlithgo could not help being impressed by Veer Savarkar's fearless personality. Talking to journalists, he said, "The brilliance of Savarkar has not dimmed in spite of long imprisonment and house arrest. Nor have his ideas changed a wee bit. On the question of war if there is one leader who has the interests of Hindus in mind, then that leader is Savarkar."

His second meeting with the Governor General took place in Simla on 5th July, 1940. In this meeting he repeated his determination about united India.

## Meets Subhash Chandra Bose

Subhash Chandra Bose was impressed by the revolutionary ideas of Veer Savarkar. So during the days of World War II, on 22nd June, 1940 all of a sudden he reached 'Savarkar Bhavan' Bombay and apprised Savarkar of his future decision to pull down the statues of Hallwell and other Englishmen in Calcutta. On this Savarkar spoke seriously, "I do not deem it proper that in the present situation of War when England is surrounded with problems and troubles, a brilliant and strong leader like you indulges in a very small agitation of pulling down the statues of Hallwell and others and consequently rots in jails."

Offering a justification for his proposed action, Subhash said, "my objective is to arouse common man's feelings against the Britishers."

"Subhash Babu! I understand the anguish in your heart, but to rot in jail for a very ordinary thing like pulling down the statues appears to me totally useless. The real politics is—keep the enemy nabbed while you are completely safe.

You may not be an armed revolutionary yourself, but your tendency is no less than that of a revolutionary. You are brilliant and far from the illusion of non-violence. That is why you do not have ideas in common with those of Gandhiji. The movement of recruiting the maximum number of Hindus in the British Indian army, which I have directed under the cover of Hindu Mahasabha, is basically a revolutionary movement."

Both the great men held a detailed and long discussion. Savarkar advised Bose not to indulge in ordinary activities, and better go abroad, direct the Indian armies trapped in Germany and Italy like Ras Behari Bose and declare India's independence. He advised Bose to free India through an armed revolution. May be Subhash Chandra Bose got from Savarkar the idea of reaching Germany and organising Indian National Army.

During meeting with Savarkar, Subhash Chandra Bose talked about his meeting with Jinnah. In this meeting Jinnah had acknowledged that Savarkar alone was the leader of the Hindus. Subhash Babu had proposed the idea of Hindu Muslim unity of Jinnah. On this Jinnah had asked, "whom do you represent when you have come for agreement?"

"I represent the Congress", spoke Subhash Chandra Bose.

"Your have been thrown out of the Congress."

"O.K. consider I represent Forward Bloc".

"Does Forward Bloc consider itself a Hindu organisation?"

"No, but as a Hindu I want to talk to you about Hindu-Muslim unity."

"The leader of Hindus at present is Veer Savarkar. You prepare him for talks. He is really competent to talk on behalf of Hindus. What's the use of talking with you unnecessarily?" Jinnah said seriously.

It is worth remembering in 1937 when Veer Savarkar was freed from Ratnagiri, *Netaji* Subhash Chandra Bose had sent him a message of congratulations. In this message he requested Veer Savarkar to join the Congress party. But in reply Savarkar wrote, "I don't believe in the principles of non-violence. I am a supporter of freedom through armed revolution. Therefore, I do not want to have contacts with any such party, which is opposed to my principles."

### The Message of Ras Behari Bose

When the illustrious patriot, Ras Behari Bose, was active in Japan, for the freedom of India, he sent to letter to Veer Savarkar through a Buddhist monk. He was organising an army with weapons and money received from Italy and Germany. He requested Veer Savarkar through this letter for co-operation in this activity. Savarkar found the proposal useful in the interest of the country. Therefore, he called upon the Hindu youths to join this army in maximum number. He criticised the friendly and opposing nations, dubbing them as imperialists. But he asked youths to join the army to take military training in the interest of the country. He put forth his proposal on the issue in the following manner: "We should formulate a policy keeping in mind the interests of the freedom of our country. From this point of view, the most appropriate and practical means available today for the defence of India and the fulfilment of our desire for freedom is the movement for militarisation. Therefore, Hindus should join the British Indian army in the largest number possible. Hindus should train themselves in battle in the battlefields of Europe and be armed."

Keeping this interest in mind, during his meeting with Lord Linlithgo, Savarkar had raised the demand for removing the ban on Hindus to be commissioned in the army, and to recruit Hindus of all castes in the armed forces. It is to be remembered that up to that time, many castes of Hindus were considered incompetent to join the army. Viceroy had assured that these demands would be met.

He was a strong supporter of converting Hindus into soldiers. He entertained a strong belief that this policy was in India's interest. Therefore, in 1940 speaking from the presidential chair of *Akhil Bharatiya Hindu Mahasabha* he opposed the Gandhian policy of non-violence, spinning wheel, *satyagraha* etc. In his opinion this policy was useless like the thought of blasting a fort with a whiff of air, rather than through ammunition. He requested people to be cautious of the Congress policy of partitioning India.

**Hyderabad Satyagraha and Savarkar**

In Hyderabad, the state of Nizam, inhuman atrocities were perpetrated on Hindus. They were not allowed to construct temples, and make *havan-kunds*. Their *janeus* were broken and they were not free to celebrate any religious festival, ceremony or *parva*. To murder Hindus and to loot their properties was a common feature there. Reading of and discourses on the *Geeta* and the *Ramayana*, and the blowing of conch or tolling the bells or any other sound in the temples were declared as illegal activities.

These atrocities of Nizam generated strong anger among Hindu public throughout the country. So, first of all, *Arya Samaj* raised a voice against these atrocities. Earlier, three brave men of *Arya Samaj* (*Arya Veer* Ved Prakash, Dharma Prakash, and Mahadev) had been murdered there. In October, 1938 Veer Savarkar reached Delhi and he held discussions with the office-bearers of *All India Arya Pratinidhi Sabha*. Later on, during the same year a *sammelan* in Sholapur was held protesting these atrocities. The president of this *sammelan* was Bapuji Anney and chief executive was Narayan Swami. Veer Savarkar also participated in this *sammelan*. In his speech he said, "The entire Hindu public of the whole country should organise itself as one unit against the inhuman atrocities of the Nizam of Hyderabad, and plunge itself into this holy war. If the poisonous hood of the religious bigotry is not smashed, then Hindus will be tortured in Bhopal and other Muslim majority areas also."

Savarkar assured Arya Samaj that Hindu Mahasabha would render total co-operation to them in their struggle against the atrocities of Nizam. In this *sammelan* first Nizam was warned that he should stop the atrocities on Hindus. When the period specified in the warning came to an end, the struggle against the Nizam began. Many Hindus were killed and many more were thrown into jails.

Veer Savarkar issued a statement to observe 22nd

January, 1939 a Nizam Protest Day. He called upon people to observe total strike on this day, hold demonstrations, pass resolutions in support of the demand and from every meeting only one voice in unison be raised to struggle for Hindu rights. As a result, Nizam Protest Day was observed throughout India, and 22nd of every month was observed as protest day till this movement and struggle continued.

Speaking from the chair of the president at the Nagpur session of Hindu Mahasabha, Veer Savarkar, criticising the atrocious policies of Nizam, called upon all Hindus to continue to struggle till the objective was realised.

The joint *satyagraha* of Arya Samaj and Hindu Mahasabha continued. Thousands of brave men participated in it, under influence of Veer Savarkar. In the end, the Nizam was forced to come to an agreement.

**Bhagalpur Struggle**

In the Madurai session of all India Hindu Mahasabha it was decided that the next session will be held at Bhagalpur, Bihar during Christmas vacations in December, 1941. At the time of this decision no one had imagined that this session would prove to be a historic event.

Preparations began for the session. Suddenly on 19th May, 1941 the Bihar government wrote to the Commissioner of Bhagalpur to inform the Hindu leaders that the Bihar government was opposed to the idea of Hindu Mahasabha holding its annual session in Bhagalpur, because on 21st December Muslims were observing their *Bakar-Id:* So, it was feared that there might be Hindu-Muslim riots. When the secretary of the Reception Committee, formed for this session, was given this notice, it was explained to him that this committee was not competent to take any decision in this regard. So the matter was referred to the meeting of *Akhil Bharatiya Hindu Mahasabha* going to be held in Calcutta. This meeting was held in June. It was unanimously decided that the session should be held in Bhagalpur only between 25th and 27th December. On 26th September Bihar government declared that under Rule 56 of the Indian Security Act, the Bihar government had decided that any session of Hindu Mahasabha cannot be held not only in Bhagalpur between 1st December, 1941 to 10th January, 1942, but also in six districts, namely Munger, Patna, Gaya, Shahabad and Muzaffarpur. Savarkar maintained contact with the Bihar government through correspondence that possibly it might take back its decision. The central executive committee of Hindu Mahasabha in Delhi decided that the session will be held in Bhagalpur between 25th and 27th December.

Veer Savarkar and the Bihar government continued exchanging letters till 5th December, 1941. Neither side was prepared to go back on its decision. Mahasabha was preparing for the session and the government was committed to stop it. The state units of Hindu Mahasabha had already elected Veer Savarkar as its national president. Though Veer Savarkar, after tendering his resignation, was prepared to make some other person president, but due to the challenge of the Bihar government, he gave up this idea. On Savarkar's call, 14th December was observed as Bhagalpur Day all over India. On this day letters from different units and places were sent to Viceroy to get the decision of the Bihar government cancelled. But the Viceroy refused to intervene saying "maintaining peace is the responsibility of the Bihar government."

Hindu Mahasabha got busy with the preparations for the session. A *pandal* was in the process of being set up at the venue of the session that the police smashed it. The police raided the office of the Provincial Mahasabha, seized and took away all the papers related to the session, and the homes of many workers were searched. As a result Bhagalpur observed a strike. The Provincial Hindu Mahasabha organised an Action Committee under the chairmanship of Pandit Raghavacharya. Pandit Raghavacharya was arrested on 17th December when he was on his way to Bhagalpur from Patna. Many persons tried to strike a compromise with the Bihar Government, but its attitude stiffened and became more strict as the date of the session neared. There was a heavy *bando bast* of police. On 23rd December, section 144 was applied to Bhagalpur. In reply the public observed hunger strike.This strike continued till 27th December. Arrests were being made on a large scale. The repressive measures of the government were at its peak. Every Hindu house was aflutter with the flag of Hindu Mahasabha. Even in the presence of the police, the sky reverberated to the sound of '*Jai Jai*' when a representative from outside alighted. The police made lathi-charge, but the enthusiasm of the public did not go down. Kumar Ganga Nand Singh, president of the Reception Committee, was put under house arrest at his residence on 23rd December itself. Many activists of Hindu Mahasabha were arrested as soon as they reached Bhagalpur. However, many representatives managed to reach Bhagalpur. Veer Savarkar left Bombay on 25th December by Bombay Mail along with many representatives. He was warmly and grandly received at many places on the way. At night he got down at Gaya station. He had to change a train there. Before his train arrived a large crowd had gathered at Gaya station and was raising slogans in his welcome. The superintendent of police of Gaya was already there with huge police force to arrest him. Showing him his arrest warrant, he was arrested. The police car look him to Central Jail. After his arrest, Veer Savarkar, in his message to Hindu Mahasabha, said, "We want peace with respect. Bhagalpur session must be held. The programme which has already been decided upon should be translated into action."

As soon as this news reached Bhagalpur, the public, not caring for section 144 and in no time, converted into a big procession. This procession passed through all the prominent places and the processionists were shouting '*Veer Savarkar ki Jai*', '*Hindu Mahasabha ki Jai*', and '*Hindustan Hinduon ki Liye*'. Big rallies were held at Shujaganj and Lajpat Park. The police again rained lathis and resorted to arrest. Prominent leaders like Dr. Naidu, Dr. Munje, Bhai Parmanand, Ashutosh Lahiri, Chandra Gupta Vidyalankar, N.C. Chatterjee, Raja Maheshwar Dayal and others were arrested. Meetings were held at many places on 24th December in Bhagalpur. At one place more than one thousand persons were arrested.

When police saw Shyama Prasad Mukherjee with a large number of representatives coming to Bhagalpur, he was stopped on his way and ordered to go back to Calcutta. But he did not carry out this order of the police. Therefore, another order of the Bihar government which banned his stay in Bihar between 25th and 27th December was read out to him. Dr. Mukherjee refused to accept this order also. On this the police arrested him on the way. Sir Gokul Chand Narang, the well known leader of Punjab, was also arrested on 25th December.

When all the leaders had been arrested, then the elderly leader of Delhi, Lala Narain Dutt, took upon his shoulders the responsibility of holding the session. Three huge rallies were held at their fixed time in Bhagalpur with the efforts of Lalaji. Besides these rallies, many small meetings were also held. In the main rallies the speeches of the President of Reception Committee, and the President of the Session were read out. Later on, the resolutions sent by the president were adopted and passed. The police got this news and it disbanded these meetings. The leaders of there meetings were also arrested.

In the Central Jail of Bhagalpur, the representatives of various states who were arrested, organised a session under the presidentship of Dr. Munje. Veer Savarkar's speech was read out here also and the resolutions despatched by him were adopted. Later on, the representatives of various provinces also delivered speeches.

On 26th and 27th December also the activities of police lathi-charge and the arrest of leaders continued. On 27th December the final meeting was secretly held in a *Dharamshala*, with twenty thousand members taking part in it. In this manner, the Bihar government, with its opposition and its police resorting to all kinds of excesses, made this session of Hindu Mahasabha, much against its wishes, famous and historic.

**Protest Against the Ban of *Satyartha Prakash***

The Muslim League, at its Karachi session, adopted a resolution asking for a ban on *Satyartha Prakash*, a good work (book) written by the founder of *Arya Samaj*, Swami Dayanand Saraswati. Mr. Jinnah proposed the bannig resolution on this book, particularly terming its 14th *samullas* going against the tenets of Islam. On 15th and 16th December a meeting of Muslim League was held in

Delhi. In this meeting, too, it put forth a demand for immediate ban by the Government of India on its above mentioned *samullas*. The cabinet of Sindh also expressed its opinion in favour of a ban on *Satyartha Prakash* but seeing the opposition by Hindus the matter was referred to the government of India. Arya Samaj also stood up in opposition to all these oppositions. It also held demonstrations in support of this book, passed resolutions and sent letters to Viceroy. On 19th and 20th February, 1944 all India session was held in Delhi. A pledge was taken here to defend and publicise *Satyartha Prakash*. Side by side three lakh rupees were collected for this work, and the government was cautioned that any decision against this holy book will result in serious consequences. Seeing this opposition, the Sindh government declared that it will not do anything in opposition to *Satyartha Prakash*. But when it observed that the Arya Samajis have become indifferent and complacent, it issued an order on 4th November that not a single copy of the book would be printed if its 14th *samullas* is not withdrawn.

It was but natural that this move would generate anger among the followers of Arya Samaj. Therefore, on 20th November, in its all India meeting of Arya Pratinidhi Sabha, it appointed and empowered Shri Ghanshyam Das Gupta to organise a committee for the defence of the book and to oppose the orders of the Sindh government. Besides, he was authorised to take all necessary steps.

Bhai Parmanand raised this issue in the Central Assembly that the above decision of the Sindh government was unjust. When a debate was in progress on the adjournment notion of Bhai Parmanand, the Congress leaders, due to their vacilallion in policy, looked askance and avoided the issue. Though this resolution could not be adopted, yet the attention of Indian public and the government was drawn towards it. Mahatma Gandhi, some Congress leaders and some neutral Muslims also crticised this order of the Sindh government.

This insult of Arya Samaj, an inalienable part of Hindu society, by the Sindh government was intolerable to Veer Savarkar. In a public meeting he declared, "So long as the ban on *Satyartha Prakash* is not lifted by the Sindh government, till then we should strongly demand a ban on *Quran* in Congress ruled states."

Later on he sent telegrams to the Governor of Sindh and Viceroy of India. He made it clear in these telegrams that the ban on *Satyartha Prakash* would generate communal envy and animosity. If the ban on *Satyartha Prakash* is not lifted, then Hindus will start an agitation to ban *Quran*. Therefore, the ban on *Satyartha Prakash* should be lifted immediately. In addition to this, Veer Savarkar met Viceroy on 27th November, 1944 with this in mind.

**Opposition to Pakistan Plan**

The Congress leaders developed an illusion that India will not attain freedom without the co-operation of Muslims. Mahatma Gandhi expressed this idea publicly also, which strengthened Jinnah's separatist policy. Finally he came out to demand Pakistan. In 1944 the Congress very strongly opposed the demand for Pakistan. Terming this demand a sin, Mahatma Gandhi declared if Pakistan was formed it would be formed on his dead body. In 1944 Rajagopalachary persuaded Gandhiji and with certain conditions attached prepared a proposal for the partition of India. He went to Jinnah with this conditional proposal, but by then the demands of Jinnah had grown still further. He did not agree to the conditions attached to the proposal and demanded complete partition. Veer Savarkar had already forecast this policy of the Congress and the obstinate adherence of Jinnah. He had cautioned Hindus to be careful with both—leaders declaring "Pakistan will be formed on my dead body" will one day accept the plan of Pakistan to please Muslims. Therefore, Hindus should not be taken in by their assurances."

When Gandhiji gave his consent to the demand for Pakistan, then the Hindu public of the country was very upset. Some nationalist Congress leaders also criticised this decision of Gandhiji. Dr. Shyama Prasad Mukherjee, the leader of Hindu Mahasabha, met Gandhiji and apprised him of the horrible long range consequences of this decision. Besides, he conveyed to him the anger and anguish of Hindus as well, but to no avail. On the call of Veer Savarkar the Pakistan plan was opposed throughout the country. Gandhiji asked Jinnah to give him some time to meet and discuss this issue. Hindus asked Gandhiji not to do this and expressed their opposition to it. Gandhiji did not care for the opposition by Hindus, went to Bombay and met Jinnah. Jinnah did not accept any of his proposals.

Veer Savarkar, who valued united India more than his own life, organised '*Akhand Bharat Neta Sammelan*' to express opposition to Pakistan plan. This *sammelan* was held on 7th and 8th October, 1944 under the leadership of Dr. Radhu Kumud Mukherjee in Delhi with great zeal. Hundreds of persons from all over India participated in it. To mention a few among them were Veer Savarkar, Dr. Radha Kumud Mukherjee, Jagadguru Shankaracharya (Puri), Shri Jamunadas Mehta, Dr. Gokul Chand Narang, Master Tara Singh, Dr. Naidu, M.C. Chatterjee, Shri Khaparde, Shri Ashutosh Lahiri, Shri Bhopatkar and Shri Veeru Mal. In this *sammelan* Veer Savarkar requested all the delegates to express their ideas with complete freedom, irrespective of the fact what their opinion was. All persons criticised the policies of Gandhi, Jinnah and Rajagopalachary and expressed their ideas in favour of the integrity and unity of India. In the end, the following resolution, supporting the integrity and unity of India, was passed unanimously:

"This *sammelan* declares that the future constitution of India should be made on the basis of integrated and free India. It declares this also that if any effort is made to destroy the integrity of India on the basis of religion, politics, economics or language, then it will be opposed at all costs with sacrifices.

"The *sammelan* expresses its total confidence in the unity and integrity of India and expresses its strong belief that the division of India will harm the country seriously. *Sammelan* requests every patriot that he faces every attempt of destroying the integrity of India by all possible means."

This *sammelan* left an extensive impact on Hindus. In 1946 the Congressmen started opposing the Pakistan plan. Then Veer Savarkar cautioned Hindus, "The Congress leaders are raising the slogan of integrated India only to gain your votes in elections. After elections they will commit breach of trust by supporting the formation of Pakistan—A vote for Congress is a vote for Pakistan." Seeing the strong opposition by Hindus, Jawahar Lal Nehru again said categorically, "The Muslim League, which has always opposed the Congress, is a communal party. We will never compromise with it, nor will we allow India to be divided."

Veer Savarkar cautioned again, "These Congress leaders are calling the Muslim League communal just to take Hindus in their fold. This is their game plan. Like Gandhi, the Congress leaders are not true to their words and assurances. Gandhi himself is sacrificing his assurances to please Muslims."

Veer Savarkar always opposed the demand for Pakistan. When the demand for Pakistan was gaining momentum, an American journalist Louis Fischer had come to India and was collecting the reactions of the people to the partition of India. He asked Savarkar, "what objection do you have to grant a separate nation, Pakistan, to Muslims?"

"Why don't you accept granting '*Negrostan*' as a separate country for them even when you see a strong demand for it?" in reply, Savarkar asked him immediately.

"Because the division of the country would be a national crime", was the reply of Louis Fischer.

On this Veer Savarkar said, "Yours is a reply imbued with strong patriotism and based on facts. No patriot will bear the partition of his country. And those who want division or partition can never be called patriots. Therefore we are opposing the plan of division of India as anti-national, whereas the followers of the Muslim League who call this country itself *Napak* (impure) are hell-bent on its division."

Louis Fishcher was highly impressed with these ideas. Later on comparing Veer Savarkar and Jinnah he wrote, "Whereas I saw limitless feeling of patriotism in the heart of Savarkar, I saw in Jinnah's heart a deep-rooted harted for India and its culture."

In spite of repeated warning by Veer Savarkar, the Hindu voters were taken in by the subtle, diplomatic moves of the Congress. The Congress won the elections, but time proved that the assurances of the Congress were lies and the warning of Veer Savarkar was correct. After winning the elections the Congress accepted the demand of Muslim League for Pakistan. On 3rd June, 1947 Jawahar Lal Nehru declared that the partition of Indian is being accepted in the interest of the permanent solution of Hindu-Muslim problem, and Pakistan came into existence on 14th August, 1947.

# In Free India

India attained freedom on 15th August, 1947, but what freedom? At what cost? And can it be called freedom in the real sense of the term? If you are released from prison at the cost of getting a part of your body amputated, then what is the significance of such a freedom? India was divided into two parts, India and Pakistan. On attaining freedom when the Congress leaders were swaying in happiness and enjoying, the whole India, and particularly Bengal and Punjab were celebrating a blood bath. In East and West Pakistan Sikhs and Hindus were butchered and killed *en masse*. Barbaric treatment was meted out to women. People, in lakhs of numbers, were leaving their homes and migrating from India to Pakistan and vice-versa.

Seeing all these events and incidents, the heart of Veer Savarkar, a sincere devotee of *Bharat Mata*, cried inconsolably. It was an unusually critical situation in which lakhs of people were coming as refugees to India from Pakistan, who had lost not only their property there but many members of their family, their kith and kin. It was not unnatural that, in consequence, a strong feeling arose among Hindus and Sikhs to seek revenge.

**Arrested for Gandhi's Assassination**

After the partition of the country twenty lakh Hindus and Sikhs were killed in Pakistan. Property worth four thousand crores was looted. Refugees, in lakhs of numbers, reached Delhi. Gandhiji held sermons daily in his prayer meetings. These refugees approached him and wanted to tell him the harrowing stories of self-experienced suffering, but instead of consoling them or sympathizing with them, Gandhiji rebuked them saying, "Go away from here. Why don't you live in Pakistan as Muslims?" The refugees returned with a lost face. But Gandhiji's conduct with

Muslims was very sympathetic. Some reaction to this violence took place in Alwar. Some Muslims from there came to Gandhiji. Gandhiji listened to them and assured them, "You will be re-habilitated in Alwar state. If this does not happen, I will undertake a fast unto death."

A little after freedom, the Pakistani *goondas* suddenly attached Kashmir. On this the Central Government warned Pakistan—if this activity is not stopped forthwith, then the sum of fifty five crore rupees due for payment to Pakistan, would be withheld. On this declaration. Gandhiji resorted to fast unto death. Some young men, dedicated to their own religion and nation, grew angry on this prejudicial policy of Gandhiji. The refugees, who had come from Pakistan, were also disappointed with this. The condition of the refugees roused the anger of youth all the more. Suddenly on 30th January, 1948 a youth named Nathu Ram Godse shot Gandhiji dead in his prayer meeting in Delhi. Nathu Ram Godse was one major activist of Maharashtra Hindu Mahasabha and he edited a weekly *Agrani* also.

On the second day of Gandhiji's assassination a huge crowd of Congressmen and Communists attacked 'Savarkar Sadan', the residence of Savarkar in Bombay. Shri Bhaskar Rao Shinde and Pathak, another young man, were with Veer Savarkar at that time. Savarkar had been ill at that time for many days. Seeing the huge crowd of attackers, Savarkar advised his only son Vishwas Rao to move out of there safely, but he refused to leave his father alone in difficulty. Though ill, Veer Savarkar prepared himself to face the aggressors. On this Pathak and Shinde stopped him from doing so, and themselves faced the aggressive crowd. The aggressors ran away in the face of resistance.

Veer Savarkar's younger brother, Dr Narayan Rao Savarkar's house was also there in the Shivaji Park area of Bombay. After attacking Savarkar Sadan, the crowd of *goondas* headed towards Dr. Narayan Rao's residence and attacked it. Later, they surrounded him and pelted stones at him till he was thoroughly drenched in blood and fell unconscious. A few days later he died.

On 31st January, the day this incident took place, the police searched his house and proposed to take Savarkar away to some other place for safety, but Savarkar rejected it saying, "I am capable of definding myself."

After this, from, 1[st] to 5[th] February the round of arrests in connexion with Gandhi *hatya-kand*, continued. Nearly twenty five thousand members of Rashtriya Swayam Sewak Sangh and Hindu Mahasabha were arrested. On 5[th] February morning Veer Savarkar was also apprehended on charges of instigating Nathu Ram Godse. When the police was about to take him away in its van, Savarkar said he wanted to visit the toilet. The Police officer was reminded of the old incident of Marseilles when Veer Savarkar was being brought from London to India and he had jumped from the window of the toilet into the sea and swam away. The police officer could not say either yes or no, but Savarkar sensed what was going on in his mind. He told him, "Don't worry, I am an old man now; and I do not consider it necessary to repeat Marseilles."

As an arrestee he was taken to Arthur Road jail in Bombay. The Congress and Communist supported newspapers now indulged in a misinformation campaign that Veer Savarkear instigated Nathu Ram Godse for the murder of Gandhiji. It was decided that the case would be conducted from Red Fort in Delhi. So Veer Savarkar was brought to Delhi and locked in Red Fort. Nathu Ram Godse, Madan Lal Pahwa, Dr. Dattatriya Purchure, Gopal Godse, Apte and Karkare and other were also lodged here.

The government appointed Shri Atma Charan as a special judge to my conduct trial of Gandhiji's murder. Among the arrested persons, the police made Shri Wange an approver, using threats, coaxing and rewards. He recorded his statement that on 17[th] January, before the assassination of Gandhiji, Godse and Apte came to 'Savarkar Sadan' to meet Savarkar, and Savarkar blessed them to be successful in the murder of Gandhi, Jinnah and Suhrawarthy' whereas Godse and Apte accepted in clear words that they did not believe that they needed someone's blessings for any work. Veer Savarkar has no hand in this assassination by any means. They murdered Gandhiji for the miserable condition of the Hindus and for the arrangement of giving fifty five crore rupees to Pakistan.

**Proved Innocent**

The public knew that Veer Savarkar has unreasonably been framed in this murder case. So a lakh rupees were collected to fight his case. Many prominent advocates of Maharashtra, Bengal, Punjab, Rajasthan, Bihar and Gujarat, notably Shri Bhopatkar, the president of Akhil Bharatiya Hindu Mahasabha, Lala Ganpat Rai, Shri Jamna Das Mehta and Shri N.P. Iyer came to argue on his behalf and fight this case.

This case started in Red Fort, Delhi at the end of the month of May. On 20th November, Veer Savarkar made a statement running into 52 pages. He categorically stated that he had been deliberaty and falsely implicated in the case. As far as the policies of Gandhiji were concerned, he was his bitter critic, but in spite of these differences he did not wish to get him (Gandhiji) murdered under any circumstances.

The police had arranged some false witnesses also. This diplomacy and obduracy was exposed before the judge himself. A false witness was brought to the court to recognize Veer Savarkar, but he could not recognize him. When he was asked to identify, then he mistook Dr. Parchure of Gwalior as Veer Savarkar. In fact, at the time of his arrest the police officer had clearly opined that he (Savarkar) was being falsely implicated in the case unnecessarily.

The case lasted for nine months. In the end on 10th February, 1949, pronounicing his judgement, the judge declared him innocent and relased him with respect. Nathu Ram Godse and Apte were sentenced to death and Gopal Godse was sentenced to life imprisonment.

On hearing the decision, Godse and the other accused did not show any symptoms of fear. They touched the feel of Veer Savarkar and raised slogans, saying, 'Integrated India, live for ever" '*Ek dhakka aur do, Pakistan Tor do*' (One more push, and destroy Pakistan).

A big crowd was waiting outside the Red Fort to hear the judgement in the case. As soon as the public knew that Veer Savarkar has been released with respect, the joy of public knew no bounds. Hindu Mahasabha wanted to take him out in a procession in a big way. Just then it was notified that a three-month ban on his entry in Delhi had been imposed. So he was sent to Bombay safe by train. People held a grand reception on his reaching here. People celebrated his release as Deepawali out of joy.

**Active Again**

Savarkar became active again for the realization of his objective, after his respectful release in the Gandhi murder case. In 1949 when the ban on Rashtriya Swayam Sewak Sangh was lifted Veer Savarkar was sincerely overjoyed. On this occasion on 15th July he sent a congratulatory message to *Sarsangha Chalak* Shri Madhav Rao Sadashiv Rao Golwalkar and expressed his desire that he (Glowalkar) would maintain the momentum of activities of the Sangh.

In 1949 the session of Hindu Mahasabha was held in Calcutta on 21st December. Dr. Narayuan Bhaskar Khare was elected its President. Though Savarkar was ill these days, he participated in it. In this session, Veer Savarkar, Dr. Khare and Shri Bhopatkar were taken out in a procession. This procession is considered unprecedented in the history of Calcutta. In this session, Veer Savarkar expressed his ideas on Hinduisation of politics and militarization of Hindus.

**Arrested Again**

In March, 1950, they started killing Hindus *en masse* in Noakhali, Dacca, Narayanganj and other places in East Pakistan. Savarkar was deeply distressed over it. Expressing his reaction he said, "Pakistan has become a headache for India for ever. It would prove dangerous for the peace and security of India."

It was at about this lime that for the safety and security of minorities in their respective area a plan for agreement between Jawahar Lal Nehru and Nawabzada Liaquat Ali, the Prime Minister of Pakistan, was drafted. Liaquat Ali was supposed to come to India for agreement. He had already bitterly criticized in Pakistan's Parliament the above mentioned speech of Veer Savarkar and the statement of Sardar Vallabh Bhai Patel regarding incidents in East

Pakistan. Before the arrival of Liaquat Ali to India, Jawahr Lal Nehru ordered the arrest of Veer Savarkar. Savarkar was in Bombay at this time. He was arrested there on 4th April, 1950. After arrest he was sent to District Jail of Belgaum. In addition to Savarkar, Shri. L.B. Bhopatkar, the ex-president of Hindu Mahasabha, Shri G.V. Ketkar, Shri Mama Rao Date, Shri G.M. Nalawade and many members of Rashtriya Swayam Sewak Sangh were also arrested.

Many institutions and newspapers of the country condemned these arrests. All of them were released a few days later.

**'Abhinav Bharat' Ends**

Veer Savarkar had founded a revolutionary institution 'Abhinav Bharat' after he passed his B.A. After the freedom of India it was felt that the institution was no longer required. Therefore, on 10th May 1952 the ending ceremony of this institution was observed in Poona. All the old revolutionaries of the country were invited. In the celebration that followed, tributes were offered to all the known as well as unknown persons who sacrificed their lives for the freedom of the country. Veer Savarkar delivered a very touching speech in this celebration. He said,

". . . we did not get freedom, it has been attained after making big sacrifices. It is completely wrong to say that we got freedom. . . To raise the military strength of the country is our first duty. Three-fourths of India has become free, that is why I am happy at heart. One-fourth of India is yet to be liberated. This is the job of young men. My Sindhu river and Sindh province have been snatched away from us. The Sindhu river which we pronounce in our morning *mantras*, we cannot forget her. Even at the cost of worth of the whole world, we will not bear the severance of relations with our Sindhu. It is our duty to liberate it.

"Hindu without Sindhu, word without meaning, body without life, all this is impossible, useless. O Sindhu river! Maharashtra has been mad in your love for a long period. There was a time when you went away from us, was separated. Then to free you from the imprisonment of dependence and bondage the mighty Maharashtrian army marched towards the north. To achieve victory in the North, Baji Rao crossed Narmada and reached upto Chambal. He conquered Delhi also. Our victorious horses drank the water of mother Yamuna, and drank the most pious milk of Ganga which enabled them to march ahead. They went across, Satluj, swam through Jhelum; they stomped over the *mlechchhas* and reached the other side of Cuttack and hoisted their saffron flag there. Their thirst for victory was quenched for a short while only after drinking to the full your most pious water, at your banks.

"O Sindhu! Mother Sindhu! Thou hast served gods. On your most pious banks our ancient most *Vidic Rishis* have performed the *Sam gayan* (elevated, religious singing) of the first *Richas* (verses) of the *Vedas*. We performed our *Sandhya vandana* with your sacred water, offered *arghya*, and accorded place to gods with limitless respect, offered tributes of the most beautiful poetic flowers. Such *Punya-salitla Maan Sindhu*! How can we forget you? Others may forget you, but this Maharashtra, Maharashtra alone will rise once more and will certainly liberate you. That is why I say,

*"Ai Sindhu! Mukta karegi tujhe*
*Maharashtra ki Raktabindu!"*

(O Sindhu! The drops of blood of Maharashtra will liberate you.)

In the course of this speech, when Veer Savarkar talked of the division of the country he became sentimental and wept inconsolably and remembering Sindhu river, his anguish of separation all of a sudden burst forth and expressed itself in a very strange manner. Seeing him weeping many in the audience found themselves weeping involuntarily.

At the end of the celebrations many revolutionaries pledged themselves for a united India. After these celebrations, for one year Savarkar went round all the cities and towns of Maharashtra and delivered lectures. The money which the public offered voluntarily in these lectures was deposited in a fund for the revolutionary memorial. Later on *Abhinav Bharat Mandir* was constructed from this fund in Nasik.

## Let Politics be Hinduised and Hindus be Militarised

The main aim of Savarkar's fight for India's freedom was the establishment of a Hindu nation. He did not believe in non-violence. He was of strong opinion and belief that for a respectable life and defence of freedom Hindus must be trained and made expert in the education for battle. The annual session of Hindu Mahasabha for the year 1955 was held in Jodhpur. Though ill, Veer Savarkar attended this session. Repeating his above principle, he said:

"India's freedom, its borders, its civilization and culture will never be safe unless the politics of the country is Hinduised and Hindus are militarized, My request to young men, my directions to them are that they should join the military in the largest number and take knowledge and training in the use of weapons, so that when required they are in a position to contribute to the freedom of the country."

## Liberation of Goa and Veer Savarkar

The government of Portugal continued to rule Goa for many years after India's freedom. Veer Savarkar suffered it as a thorn in his flesh and wondered why India did not take Goa in its fold. Savarkar was the fist to raise voice for the liberation of Goa. He said in the Ahmedabad session of Hindu Mahasabha:

"We want total freedom of India. The very pronouncement of 'French Hindustan', 'Portgese Hindustan' is intolerable to our ears and is a sign of our foolishness. We should take a pledge to create an integrated and united India, by completely ending this artificial and forced political division. We Hindus should declare with confidence that only an integrated, unified and united India (from Kashmir to Rameshwaram, and from Sindhu to Assam) is acceptable to us. We should struggle to liberate Goa, Pondicherry etc. from Portugese domination."

In 1946, too an agitation was made for the liberation of Goa. In 1955, a few days after the Jodhpur session of Hindu Mahasabha, a movement for the liberation of Goa started. The batches of *satyagrahis* from all over the country started moving to Goa. Hindu Mahasabha, Jan Sangh,

Ram Rajya Parishad etc. jointed this movement. A group of Hindu Mahasabha from Meerut made a brief stay at Bombay to meet Veer Savarkar and receive his blessings for their expedition. This group included Shri Vinod, the editor of daily '*Prabhat*' (Meerut). He discussed the matter with Veer Savarkar. On this Veer Savarkar said:

"You have come from Meerut, the land of revolution, and are going to Goa with an intention to liberate it, being shot at, killed ad sacrificed in the process. This is an ample indicator of your patriotism but that you present yourself unarmed before the armed Portugese demons is a policy which I did not consider correct in the past, nor do I consider correct now. When you have the spirit of sacrifice in your hearts, why don't you go armed with rifles in your hand? Go armed with weapons and get killed after killing the enemy –The government should hand over to the army the job of liberating Goa. Goa will be freed by armed military action. You will attain success through *shastragraha* instead of through *satyagraha*."

Veer Savarkar's forecast came tune. *Satyagrahi* batches went there again and again. But finally the Government of India was forced to dispatch its armies there, and through their action, Goa was liberated in 1961. Veer Savarkar was very happy to hear this news. Though ill, he got up and hoisted saffron flag at his residence.

Veer Savarkar had contributed to the movement to liberate Kashmir also. When this movement started under the leadership of Dr. Shyama Prasad Mukherjee, he ordered the Executive Committee of Hindu Mahasabha that it should render assistance to Dr. Shyama Prasad Mukherjee, in this movement. As a result, Hindu Mahasabha sent its 600 activists to joint this movement. Dr. Mukherjee was arrested in this movement and later he died inside the jail. Veer Savarkar was seriously saddened by this untimely death of Dr. Mukherjee. It is evident that Veer Savarkar worked thoughout his life for an integrated and united India.

**Tilak Birth Centenary Celebrations**

In 1956 the Birth Centenary of Tilak was celebrated all

over India with great zeal and respect. Ceremonies and programmes were held all over. Veer Sarvakar addressed Tilak birth centenary celebrations in Poona. His speech was tape- recorded.

Lokmanya Tilak was a strong opponed of the weak policies of the Congress Party. He was in total disagreement with Congress over its useless policy of Muslim appeasement. Earlier on 28th May in 1946 also the Hindu Mahasabha had celebrated his 90th birthday with zeal in Amravati. On this occasion Veer Savarkar was presented with a purse of three lakh rupees as gift. On this occasion, someone asked him, "Why did you reject joining Congress when your source of inspiration, Lokmanya Tilak, was in Congress?"

Replying this question, Veer Savarkar said, "It is true that *Mahatma* Tilak was in Congress, and it is also true that the Congress of Tilak did not act in a partisan manner with anybody. 'Weightage' used not to be given in those days and partistism too was not commercialized. "Freedom is impossible without non-violence", this mad phrase was not uttered by anybody in those days. *Mahatma* Tilak was in Congress, and I learnt patriotism from him, and I am following his instructions in this respect right upto this day. I am sure I have not adulterated his principles ever. I have always favoured to come out fearlessly and speak in a non-partisan manner. Hindu Mahasabha is totally following his footprints and policies. Had Congress continued to follow the polices of *Mahatma* Tilka, I would have joined it happily."

**Centenary Celebrations of 1857 Fight for Freedom**

On 10th May, 1957 the centenary of 1857's first fight for India's freedom was celebrated. A special celebration on this occasion was held in Delhi in Deevan Hall of Arya Samaj Mandir on behalf of Arya Samaj. The convernor of these celebrations was Lala Ram Gopal Shalwale (at present President), the secretary of the then All India Arya Samaj Sabha. Veer Savarkar was accorded a very warm and respectable reception in this celebration. That very day, in Ram Leela Maidan, in a public meeting organized for his civic reception, in reply to his welcome, Veer Savarkar expounding the importance of military power, said,

"We have two ideals before us. One ideal is that of Buddha, and the other is that of battle. We will have to choose one of these - Buddha or *yuddha*. It depends on our foresight whether we accept the suicidal policy of Buddha or the policy of battle leading to victory."

At one stage during this speech, he expressed the following ideas, "Right upto this day whoever has supported me has received either *Kala-pani* or deportation or hanging. I could not arrange anything more than this to anybody. I do not know what you expect from me when you think of me. I am happy over this fact that I have achieved in my lifetime the objective that I set before myself. The Englishmen have left this place, and India is independent. To keep the freedom of the country safe and intact and to take it to the heights of prosperity is the work of the people. As far as I am concerned, I am not sorry for my fate."

Next day on 11th May, Veer Savarkar invited the workers of Hindu Mahasabha over light refreshments. On this occasion he praised those workers who steadfastly followed their principles under most adverse circumstances, and advised them to march ahead with confidence for the formation of an integrated and united India. He said,

". . . you deserve thanks that you are standing committed under the Hindu banner in these difficult and adverse circumstances. I could not give anything to those who accepted me as leader and suffered humiliation and poverty and difficulties for strengthening Hindu society for the last 20 years. You are with me even after sacrificing each and everything you had. I am happy to see your steadfastness, determination and commitment to principles. March ahead with this flag in your shoulders. I know that his struggle is not easy. But I am a perfect optimist, and not a pessimist. You march ahead with full confidence and hope. Final victory is ours. I want only this that each one of you think that even if you are all alone, even then you will continue to struggle for the re-establishment of an integrated and united Hindu nation."

**Veer Savarkar *Mrityunjaya* Celebration**

Veer Savarkar was sentenced to two life sentences in December, 1910 and January 1911. Fifty years passed since this incident took place. When these sentences were pronounced, nobody hoped that he would return to India and he was still more lucky to see India attain freedom. Hindu Mahasabha organized Veer Savarkar *Mahamritunjaya* celebrations on 24th December, 1960 in the whole India, and on 15th January in Poona on this occasion to relive happy memories. All the political parties joined these celebrations, forgetting their personal and principles related differences.

In these celebrations the famous socialist leader Shri S.M. Joshi, *Senapati* Bapah, Shri Bhau Rao Modak, Shri Ketkar, Shri Jayant Rao Talak the grandson *Lokmanya* Tilak delivered speeches appreciating the personality of Veer Savarkar and praising his actions. All the leaders called Veer Savarkar an undefeated soldier-leader of India's fight for freedom and wished him a long life. At other places, people were all praise in their speeches for the actions of Veer Savarkar.

**Reaction on Attack by China**

Veer Savarkar was repeatedly expressing himself in favour of more and intense militarisation, but the political leaders of India, shouldering its responsibility, did not pay any heed to him. Prime Minister Pandit Jawahar Lal Nehru was busy harping on *Panchsheel* and world peace. By striking friendship with China, he thought that no country would attack a peace loving India. Veer Savarkar had informed in advance the government of India that so much trust on China was misplaced. Besides this, in a rally in Poona, he had warned the government of India to remain cantious vis-a-vis China. His statement was published under the title '*Upekshit Vani*' in all the prominent papers of Hindi, English and Marathi languages, but the authorities deeply engrossed in the intoxication of power, completely ignored it, and finally in 1962 China attacked India.

Aged revolutionary leader Savarkar was ill in those days. He was deeply distressed at heart when he heard the news of this war. Expressing his reaction on this occasion he said, "Had the men in power, lost under the illusion of non-violence *Panchsheel* and world peace, accepted my advice and first militarized the whole nation, our brave and chivalrous army would have driven the Chinese back upto Peking and shattered their power illusion. But I don't know for how long these 'great men', riding on the imaginary flight of non-violence and world peace, would continue to put national honour on the list of non-violence?"

Veer Savarkar hated useless idealism. So he strongly criticized the policy of 'we will not make atom bomb' of the government of India. Declaring this policy highly harmful for the country, he said, "Indian administrator should understand it well that in the present period one who has a strong army (power) has his rule secure." This principle is alone practical. If our enemy China is armed with atom bomb, and hydrogen bomb, then we should go on trying to make more powerful bombs to face it. 'We will never make an atom bomb', this declaration shows our foolishness and cowardice only."

Shri Krishna Menon was the Defence Minister of India at the time of attack by China. It is said about his that he was a covert Communist. India faced defeat in the aggression. The Chinese army crossed Indian border and came deep inside. So he was removed from his post and Yashwant Rao Balwant Rao Chavan was made the Defence Minister. Congratulating him on his appointment, Veer Savarkar wrote:

"You are a resident of Maharashtra, the land of the brave. Therefore, I believe that in our Defence department under your leadership the country would immediately adopt the policy of strength and steadfastness and would be fully capable of defending the freedom of the nation."

The eyes of the government of India were opened after the Chinese aggression. It decided to increase its military strength. Veer Savarkar was happy with this decision. He said, "Develop and army of a minimum of twenty five lakh regular soldiers and arm it with the latest arms and weapons." Along with this he advised the government to impart compulsory military training to every youth.

When this war with China started then many Congress leaders realized the importance of repeated warnings given by Veer Savarkar earlier. The then Governor of Maharashtra, Shri Shri Prakash, who was highly impressed by the warning given by Veer Savarkar through his article entitled '*Upekshit Vani*' without caring for the displeasure or anger of the Central leadership, came to meet him a few days after the war with China. He acknowledged the significance of that article and praised Veer Savarkar for his foresightedness.

### Financial Help by the Government

Veer Savarkar had sacrificed everything to free his motherland. The freedom of his motherland was the only objective he pursued, and he never expected anything in return. In fact, he was a *nishkam karmayogi* (a man of action, without any expectation). Even after the freedom of the country, the persons who assumed power did not give him the honour which he deserved in every respect. It was in 1965 that the Maharasthra and the Central Government gave his some financial help, whereas other freedom fighters whose renunciation and sacrifice were just negligible when compared to Veer Savarkar were granted pensions and other facilities much earlier. Many of them were enjoying the spoils of power on junior and higher ranks. Even after the grant of much delayed financial help, demonstrating his narrow mentality Abid Ali Jaffer Bhai, a Member of Parliament, raising an objection on this issue, demanded in Parliament, "Why is the government giving financial help to Savarkar?" On this the government had to admit, "We consider him a freedom fighter."

### Reaction on Attack by Pakistan

After the Chinese aggression in 1962, Pakistan attacked India in 1965. Lying on the patient's bed, the heart of Veer Savarkar cried in anguish when heard this news, and lambasted the Congress policy of appeasement, and carelessness vis-à-vis Pakistan. Shri Lal Bhadur Shastri was the Prime Minister at that time. The Indian army scored good success, in the wake of competent war policy of this Prime Minister. Our army chased the Pakistani force through Dograi, Kargil and Hajipir passes and landed straight at Lahore.

At the time of this aggression, the 82 years old and ill Savarkar regularly read the newspapers. When he read the news of advance and victory of Indian armed forces, his heart leapt up with joy. Lying on his bed and pointing towards the map of India on the wall he would say, "The enemy on this spot will be entrapped by us. If our victorious forces marked ahead a bit more quickly and once captured Lahore, then not to talk of Rawalpindi, we can march (*mandi mar sakte hain*) right upto Kabul and conquer it."

This devotee of integrated India saw in these victories the possibility of the realization of his dream of integrated and united India. It appeared to him that his desire 'my funeral rites should be performed on the banks of Sindhu river' will be fulfilled. Therefore, he immediately congratulated Lal Bahadur Shastri and advised him to take the revenge of the mistake of partition of India:

"Now the time has come that we corrected the mistake of partition of India in 1947."

Indian army was continuously winning and marching forward when all of a sudden it received orders of ceasefire. The advancing footsteps of the Indian brave soldiers stopped. Veer Savarkar called this decision of the Government of India foolish and suicidal. All his happiness disappeared. He underwent a great mental blow. His anguish came out in this reactrion:

"The *Vijaishree* (trophy of victory in war) which thousands of Hindu youths obtained by sacrificing themselves will be lost by these Gandhiite leaders. Entertaining any hope from them is useless."

The stroke that Veer Savarkar suffered due to this disappointment proved fatal to this man in his old age.

# Everlasting Sleep

Aged body, continuing unwell for many years and the stoppage of Indian soldiers marching towards victory—all this made Veer Savarkar ill in a very serious way. Death is inevitable now—thinking this in illness he gave up even taking medicines after the Tashkent Agreement. It was natural that the members of the family would be worried in a situation of this kind. They tried all kinds of things to persuade Savarkar to take medicine, but could not succeed. Dr. Sathe was his intimate friend and personal physician. He was treating him at this time. All the members of the family were disappointed at Savarkar's insistence on not taking medicine. All were in a fix and did not know what to do. They were obliged to administer him medicine somehow. Vishwas Savarkar, the son of Veer Savarkar, nephew Vikram Savarkar and personal secretary Bal Savarkar decided to mix medicine in his tea and give it to him in this way. So on doctor's advice medicine was mixed in tea and given to him. But Savarkar suspected it, and therefore he refused to take tea, "You give medicine in tea. Fine. I'll not take tea also. Now I do not want to live. What do I have to do by keeping alive? I have already discharged what I thought was my duty."

In spite of all this, Dr. Sathe examined him from outside regularly. One day he said to Dr. Sathe, "Sathe! I do not need medicinal treatment now. You are very close to me and are my doctor also. I have accepted all your advice right upto this day. Now you accept my last wish. Kindly give me now such medicine so that I need not talk after that."

Dr. Sathe suffered indescribable pain on hearing these words from Veer Savarkar, the devotee of integrated and united India.

On hearing the news of Savarkar's illness, Jagadguru Shankaracharya of Dwarka Peeth himself came to 'Savarkar

Sadan' to have his *darshan*. This great freedom fighter welcomed and honoured him, lying on his bed. Thousand of his friends and admirers came to enquire about his health. Everybody's heart was filled with emotions and sentiments when they saw this brave man lying in bed.

### Final Departure

Veer Savarkar's condition continued to deteriorate and on 26th February 1966 morning it was apparent that the end was near. Doctors were busy performing their duty. Oxygen was administered and injections were given, but to no avail. At about 11.00 a.m. Veer Savarkar departed for his final journey, went into everlasting sleep.

The entire Hindu world was plunged into grief on hearing the news of the extinguishing of this flame which spread around the light of freedom. A rare personality of the world, who considered all the worldly pleasure too small and spurned them, one who took the thorny path of revolution to safeguard the glory of his motherland, a person before whom all the impediments of the world surrendered and bowed their head seeing his irrepressible patriotism and zeal—it is but certain that when mother India saw this rare and chivalrous man sleeping in eternal sleep she too cried silently. One who always took pledge himself and made others also to take a pledge to liberate Sindhu river and Sindhu province, in the grief on the demise of that noble son undoubtedly *punya salita Sindhu*, too, must have cried quietly in its unexpressed beating of waves in its ever gurgling moan.

In his lifetime Veer Savarkar had given clear instructions that on his death there should be no strike, no stoppage of work, nothing of the kind, because all these things harm the nation.

### Mammoth Crowd for His Last *Darshan*

Veer Savarkar's body covered with flowers was placed in one room of the 'Savarkar Sadan' for the visitors. On this day none had to ask others as to where the 'Savarkar Sandan' was. It seemed that the entire Bombay city was converging on to that point. Huge crowd of humanity, unusually quiet, silent and in a disciplined form was passing through there to see its beloved freedom fighting leader. There was a nearly half mile long queue of old freedom fighters. Among these visitors (*darshanarthis*) were the old, aged, middle aged, youths, adolescents, children, men and women. All faces were sad, all hearts were grief-stricken, all heads filled with faith, respect and awe. All eyes were moist at permanent separation from their dear Veer Savarkar. Some were wiping their tears, some were sobbing, some were lost in deep thoughts on seeing his physical body and there were some others who cried and wept inconsolably.

What an irony! One who thundered with his words of freedom, that matchless brave person has fallen silent for ever. One who, throughout his life, traversed on this thorny path of revolution, well, his physical body was all covered with flowers.

**Funeral Procession**

His body was kept for the *darshan* by visitors from 26th February noon to 3.00 p.m. on 27th February. Preparations began after 3.00 for taking out the funeral procession. A specially decorated truck, which had an old cannon on its top in front, and two cannons, one on each side, was brought to 'Savarkar Sadan'. Savakar's body was placed on it. People and visitors who were present there raised slogans, '*Veer Savarkar Amar Rahe*' (Veer Savarkar will live for ever), '*Swatantrya Lakshmi ki Jai*' (Hail the Goddess of Freedom), and '*Hindu Rashtra ki Jai*' (Hail Hindu nation). When Veer Savarkar's body draped in the flag of Hindu Mahasabha was being placed on the truck, Bombay Mayor Madhavan garlanded it. The funeral procession started from his residence, 'Savarkar Sadan'. Many important persons had lined on the way. Among them were the famous film director and producer, V. Shanta Ram, the leader of opposition in Maharashtra Legislative Assembly Shri Gomte, Acharya P.K. Attrey and others. Earlier in the morning many prominent political leaders, intellectuals and other persons from different fields had come to visit, pay their respects and have Savarkar's last *darshan*. Among them the names of Bala Saheb, a Minister of the Maharashtra

State, Dr. R.V. Sathe, the Vice-Chancellor of Bombay University, Dr. Pitke, the Director of Maharashtra Rublicity Department, P.K. Sawant, Shri Bhau Rao Modak, the trustee of *Kesari* and George Fernandes, the famous Socialist leader, are worth mentioning.

The funeral procession started. A big oil painting of Veer Savarkar was also placed on the truck carrying his dead body. A huge crowd of two lakh persons followed it. On the right and left, front and back, i.e. on all sides of the truck posters with slogans such as '*Veer Savarkar Amar Rahe*', '*Hindu Dharma ki Jai*', and '*Hindu Rashtra ki Jai*' were pasted. People in the funeral procession were shouting these slogans in sky-piercing, loud voice. The loudspeaker placed on the truck was amplifying there slogans. In front of the funeral procession walked Nitya Narayan Banerjee, the president of Hindu Mahasabha, Shri Bachchharaj Vyas, the leader of Bharatiya Jan Sangh and Shri Dange, the Communist leader. As the funeral procession moved ahead, more and more persons joined it. Many people were already waiting on the way to have *darshan* of late Veer Savarkar. People of all hues, religions and castes had gathered on both sides of the road and taken positions on footpaths, in shops, on raised platforms, on roofs, in windows, door, wherever they could find a vantage point. In funeral procession, on both sides, volunteers, wearing saffron coloured Swastika printed bands on their arms, were walking in a formal queue.

The fureral procession, starting form Shivaji Park, wound its way through Ranade Road, Kelkar Road, Tilak Bridge, Lal Bagh and then reached Saat Rasta. From there it reached Chandanwadi Crematorium, passing through Bombay Central, Grant Road, Opera House and Girgaum Road.

**Cremation**

It was evening by the time the funeral procession reached Chandanvadi. Here his dead body was taken down from the truck that carried it, and Shri Nitya Narayan Banerjee, Acharya P.K. Attrey, Shri Bachchharaj, G.S. Sardesai and others paid their final Tributes to the late revolutionary leader. After that the dead body of Veer Savarkar was placed in the electrical crematorium. In a very short time the high voltage of electricity of the crematorium reduced the dead body of this matchless, brilliant personality to a handful of ashes.

**The Will of Savarkar**

To compare Veer Savarkar with somebody else is just to minimize his significance. He had dedicated everything he had to the nation. He was a synonym for the love of country. His will confirms that he could easily bear personal loss, but it was almost intolerable for him to bear the national loss. He believed that after his death, his followers will call for a *bandh* or strike. All this will harm the country financially. Therefore, he had clearly told the people close to him that after his death no *bandh* or strike be resorted to. Along with this he had asked his family not to waste money unnecessarily on *sharddha*. More than his *Sharddha* he was worried for the publicity of Hindu *dharma*. So he arranged and kept apart some money for this purpose. Important extracts form his will are as follows:

"No strike should be observed on my death. Nor any activity of any kind be undertaken which results into harm to the country. Money likely to be spent on my *sharddha* should be saved and given to Hindu religious institutions in charity. I am gifting Rs five thousand from my personal cash to *shuddhi* movement. Hindus should carry on with the *shuddhi* movement in an appropriate manner."

'The nation should not be harmed even after my death'—such noble ideas can be entertained by a great man of Savarkar's stature only. Head he not given these instructions it was possible that the anger of youths found expression in protesting against the government for the treatment it had meted out to Veer Savarkar.

# Hindu, Hindu Nation and Hindutva

Veer Vinayak Damodar Savarkar was a unique person in Indian history, in India's revolutionary movement. He was different from the kind of politicians these days. He would speak out frankly and with boldness whatever he thought right. Integrated and united India, Hindu, Hindi, Hindustan— the expressions which the leaders of today shun were the *mool-mantras* (*summum-bonum*) of life for Veer Savarkar. He had specially, and in his own original way, thought about religion, politics, nation, culture, civilization and society. A man's thought about a subject or his point of view is called his philosophy of life about that. Savarkar's philosophy of life is *Hindutvavadi* philosophy. The objective of his revolutionary life was the protection of Hindu culture, its dissemination and extension, and the defence of undivided Hindu nation. His philosophy of life is clearly reflected in the books be wrote, activities he undertook and the speeches he delivered from time to time. One does not have to use one's imagination to understand his philosophy of life.

Veer Savarkar is a concrete form of ideas imbued with *Hindutva*. His entire life is replete with these ideas. In earlier chapters his ideas have been mentioned in the context of incidents. In fact, it appears nearly impossible to keep his life separate from his philosophy of life. In the present section the main elements of his philosophy of life are being considered. In the first chapter is the description of Hindu, *Hindutva* and Hindu nation. In other chapters, there is a presentation in abridged form of his speeches delivered from time to time at sessions of Hindu Maha Sabha. It is absolutely necessary to understand Veer Savarkar's philosophy of life in order to understand him.

**Hindu**

India remained under the rule of others/foreigners for hundred of years due to a cycle of time. As a result it developed many orthodoxies. Later on Hindus developed an attitude of indifference towards their religion, nation and society due to the machinations of foreigners and people of other faiths. As a result, people felt ashamed of calling themselves Hindus. In this context, Veer Savarkar states:

"Among the persons who are asking questions, quite a few have doubts whether they are Hindus or not.

"Why should I call myself a Hindu?" Among the persons asking this questions, some are cheap persons loitering around the military camp of Hindu nation. The real life of Hindu nation is not the persons who lay down their lives at the time of crisis, but those brave persons who run away changing themselves as soon as the crisis overtakes the country. Shall we get more seats in Legislative Council by remaining Hindu or by becoming non-Hindu? Their remaining a Hindu or a non-Hindu depends on the arithmetic to that question. If they asked, "Why should I remain a Hindu?", then the simple answer to that question is, "it is better that you remain a non-Hindu." The reason is that you interpret *Hindutva* as a means only to get money. Go and become a non-Hindu as soon as you can. The reason is that today it is non-Hindu who are getting more jobs and four annas to fill their stomachs. When the time of we Hindus come then these slaves of their belly would come under the banner of Hindu saying "why should I not be a Hindu?"

**Hindutva**

*Hindutva* is a liberal way of life. To take it as a religion like Islam or Christianity would be a mistake because the rules of religion in the case of other religions are written in their religious books. This is not the case in respect of Hindu religion. Veer Savarkar clearly held that the characteristics of *Hindutva* are not written in any particular book.

"Which interpretation of *Hindutva* do we find correct and useful? One thing is certain. *Hindutva* is not in a particular turban, or in *Brahma-sutra*, in tuft of hair on the head or in cow's urine. *Hindutva* is not a book written on parchment of palm tree, which will break into pieces as soon as the palm leaf falls and crashes, nor is it an incident written on paper, which is born today and will be destroyed tomorrow. *Hindutva* is not a suggestion or proposal put forward at a Round Table Conference. *Hindutva* is the life of a great race. It is a culmination of untiring labour and efforts of holy souls, sacrificed and martyred individuals over thousands and thousands of years and ages. It is on decline today, still it is an ocean. It is a crater full of lava, though appears sleeping at present. That *Virat rashtra pusush* (mighty nation) is working through involuntary jerks and performing blessed (*Prasad*) deeds. But this unconscious state is directed upwards, it is not death. Those hundreds and thousands of sacrificed and martyred souls whose every pore of body is eager even today to dedicate itself for the elevation of Hindu religion and Hindu nation, the anguish and *atma-yagna* of those sacrificed souls is a proof of composite and perennial life of Hindu nation. They are calling for its renaissance and resurgence."

It is evident that for Veer Savarkar *Hindutva* means the original inhabitants of this place.

**Hindu Nation**

What are the characteristics of a nation? Why Hindu nation? What is its identity? Is the idea of a Hindu nation in conflict with a universal or world nation? The following lines of Veer Savarkar offer explanation to these issues:

"Is there, in reality, a concept like Hindu nation? There are persons who, while asking this question in categorical terms, are asking about the religious bonds or other worldly bonds of *Hindutva* as well. We want to ask of the authentic intellectuals among foreigners, we want them to tell us what are the special or particular constituents of the countries such as England, Germany, Italy, Japan, Ireland etc. It these constituents are available with the same intensity in the formation of Hindu nation, then you will have to accept the existence of Hindu nation also. Otherwise we will have to get out of the whole debate saying that there is nothing like a nation in the whole world. There are some elements also in that statement. The entire human race is one nation, the whole earth is one country and the whole humanity is one religion—this, too is an aim. We are not in dispute with it. But whenever you bring that aim into common practice, then at that time you will realize that the signature on the pledge of the first citizen, if ever that happens, will be that of this Hindu race, this Hindu nation. It was saint Tuka Ram who said '*Hamara Swadesh, bhuvan traya mein vas*' (Our country, it is spread over all the three spheres, the netherland, the earth and the space), and it was a Hindu, Advaitacharya Shankar who was explained '*Varanasi Medini*'. But every big or small race of the world wants to make its own, separate and independent group as a nation and wants to exploit and plunder others. Till then Hindu nation also wants to maintain its independent existence.

"How did the English, French, Japanese and American principalities get the right to assume undisputed status as a nation? What is your opinion in this respect? Nationality may or may not have other constituents, even then the foremost constituents is place only. Isn't it? The Englishmen have England, the French have France, the Germans have Germany, the Russians have Russia, i.e. these people in these areas are an integrated and majority population and have been traditionally living there over a number of years. So a specific father land, native land is with them. If this factor offers them the candidature/objectivity to be called a nation, then the foremost constituent of nationality is place. See it in India's context. The place of our Hindu race, this Hindustan is our native land. . . it has been traditionally the abode of Hindus. This extensive country, this native land of ours, of Hindus. Let us call it our father land. This 'Hindustan' should be and remain Hindustan."

A language and a script are the other characteristics of nationality. We Hindus do not lack in it in any form. Our, Hindus' common *dharma*-language Sanskrit and common *dharma*-script *devnagari* had been established and standardized for many centuries. For crores of *Vedic*

*Sanatani* people it is virtually the divine language. The somber and vast literature of our Jain, Buddha, Arya and other religious sects is embedded and embellished in that language. The famous tenth Guru of Sikhs, Shri Govind Singh Ji, deliberately sent his disciples to Kashi to study Sanskrit and formed an intellectual class of *Nirmal* Sikhs. His own, entire tenth scripture of Guru Govind Singh ji is written in *nagari* script in Hindi language. From Kashmir to Maharashtra many Sanskritised languages of crores of Hindus are enriched at the level of this *dev-vani* (Sanskrit)....

"This Sanskrit language, this national language of ours, of Hindus, is not your or my creation, or of one or two generations. It is rather the result of dispassionate and perennial efforts of many generations of *pandits*, saints and *mahants*, right from *Vedarshis* to Swami Dayananad and whose efforts have secured for this language of salvation the status of *rashtra-bhasha* (national language). Just as we Hindus have *dharma*-language and script in Sanskrit and *nagari*, similarly our practical *rashtra-bhasha* is Hindi and *rashtra-lipi* is *nagari*.

"If due to a common past, common living and common sharing of joys and griefs over two hundred years time can grant to many ancestries, races and languages as those in America, with its many differences the status of one living nation, then we, Hindus, too, have a more than two thousand years old history of common, important and splendid past which stands amidst us rock solid like the Himalayas. This is in addition to, or if we do not take into reckoning the legendry period of Ram and Krishna, the period of *Shrutis* and the period of *Ramayana* and *Mahabharata*. Due to this reason the Hindu race certainly meets the criterion of language and common living and a united nation.

"Divided into seven nationalities, again and again defeated by the attacks of Danes, Dutch, English and Normans, getting drenched with blood repeatedly through the war of Roses and Jews, if the history of England as a nation based upon language, culture, country and objectives; then the last two thousand years' history of we Hindus, which has been undivided, common, great significant and grand, is strong and competent enough to entitle our past as our national past. Barring China, not other present nation in the world is lucky to have such a historic asset.

"I normally do not mention the bonds of common religion forming the fundamental bases of Hindus as a united nation. This factor is eminently significant in combining crores and crores of people in one group and initiating them into the strength of common holy land, particularly in the background of psychological development of human race today. The intellectuals will find no objection, since this fact is directly proved and revealed to them. Therefore, it become important to consider this factor as well. All Muslims offer *namaz* with their faces towards Mecca. When the holy land is common, then many opposing and unrelated castes, too, unite and rise together. The kings, princes and rulers of Europe, though being at loggerheads with one another, almost daggers drawn, united and fought for a hundred years over Palee time. Only for this reason, it was their holy land, the land of their religious order, the land of their prophet. There would hardly be one or two lucky races like Hindus who, in the context of this holy land, have religion as the most potent uniting and strengthening factor for organized nationality. The reason is that what is our fatherland is also our holy land, our religious land as well. All the Hindus, whether they are *Sanatani*, Sikh, Jains or Lingayats, Arya or Bauddha, have one fatherland, one holy land. So from Sindh to non-Sindh it is one India, *Bharat Varsha*. When there is one country, then countries and districts too become one living entity. Jews and Muslims can be together and united just on the common base of having one holy land. Since our father land and holy land are one and the same of Hindus, then we are one living unit, one life, one nation certainly. . . . The names of we Hindus are common . . . Through a common religious code, *Karma-Kand*, the life of crores of Hindus is regulated in general. See *Deepawali*. From Bengal to Sindh, from Nepal to Madras, the whole Hindu, Hindustan shines in brilliance of light in one episode of time. *Bhaiyaduj*: In every home a sister is wishing her brother well through an emotional, tearful lamp of love. This *Gokul Ashtami*. This vast country, almost the size of a continent, crores of Hindus—this entire nation of thirty crore Hindus, with *gulal* and *kheel* in hands, waits eagerly upto the middle of night like mother Devki for the time of birth of Lord Krishna. And on Lord's birth, the joy of crores of Hindus surges up simultaneously from Kashmir to Kanya Kumari. On *Rang Panchami*, boys and girls from the poor man's hut to the kings and princes with golden crowns and seats in their hands—the whole India can be seen red in colour, flying and showering colour and *gulal* on one another. Even if you keep apart the religious feelings associated with these festivals, even then the whole India becomes one, socially, imbued with the spirit of this celebration. If this land cannot be called a nation, then we will be forced to state that there is nothing like a nationality culture anywhere in the world.

"Like common place the strength of population is also called a characteristic of nationality, but to ask Hindus to produce a certificate to that effect would be like asking *Kuber* to provide surety. There are people who did not have countries of their own, or even if they had then their countries were not in their control for centuries, and who can be called *one* on the basis of unity of culture and language only. Examples are Poland, Hungary, Romania, Spain and Portugal. If the strength of a crore or less population can entitle them to be a nation, then the strength of population of this Hindu race, of strong and orthodox Hindus (barring cheap people) is thirty crore. One country, one language, one script, one history, one past, one future one culture, one father land, one holy land—this Hindu nation of thirty crore people, bound and intertwined in relations in the greatest among great nations of the world."

In his above discourse, Veer Savarkar proved on the strength of his convincing proof that Hindus are one nation from all angles, because they had a definite place to live for centuries, they had an ancient language and a script, had a common glorious past; their religions were born in this land; their ancestors lived here; they had a common culture and that they do not lack in the strength of population.

## We Hindus Are One Nation

Here Veer Savarkar has offered more evidence and explained in detail: Why a Hindu nation is required? How the Hindu race (nation) has maintained its existence for the last two thousand years? How the Hindu religion has defended and extended itself by assimilating foreigners in itself?

"It is that great bond. We want a Hindu nation, that is why we Hindus are one nation. We have to live with the name of Hindus and we like to die with that name. That is why we are Hindus. Just as river comes first and the bridge later, likewise desire comes first, nation first, and explanation later. Alexander came from Grace and cut *Brahmins* to pieces. The Muslims beheaded Guru Tegh Bahadur. When a saw was placed on Mati Das's head and even then he did not agree to give up his religion, he was *sawed* into two in vertical (standing) position. The flesh of Banda Veer was torn to pieces by piercing hot iron rods into his body. Shambhaji's eyes were mutilated through piercing and his tongue was cut out. Har Pal was skinned alive. These brave men who pulled their tongues out and killed themselves so that their religion is not changed at the hands of Tipu–were the actions of these courageous persons performed so that you do not undertake a bookish explanation or make a grammatical mistake or any other mistake of language? No, absolutely not! They did not love any life other than *Hinutva*, they did not want to live — '*Dharma hetu sir diya, par shirah na diya*' (They offered their head for religion but did not give up their religion). Their strong and burning desire (for *Hindutva*) is the explanation of their *Hindutva*, their *Hindutva* is their grammar.

"O Hindus! If our nation has survived for two thousand long years, has it been by chance? No. Those who say so are either foolish or crooked. We survived, because we were the most capable to survive. Whatever was required to be forgotten in those circumstances, we forgot that; and learnt what was required to be learnt. Therefore, we overcame those circumstances and survived.

"Alexander came conquering the world. He had much more than what we possessed. He attacked us according to his strategy, but soon Chandra Gupta and Chanakya swallowed him along with his strategy and organization of weapons. Whatever was weak at our end, was taken out, strengthened and perfected.

"Strategically organising and increasing our combatant power, we not only drove him to the other side of Sindhu river, we beat and chased him out, beyond Hindukush. Huns came. Shak came. They had smashed half of Europe and the whole Asia. We fought against them for two centuries, developed new weapons, conducted required research and brought out the things that we needed to defeat them. And by adopting new strategies and weapons be headed their most powerful emperor. One after another, we blew to smithereens the Shaks a number of times. Vikramaditya and kings in his lineage created the legends of defeating *Shak* and *Hun* enemies, and built victory towers of Indian victory at a number of places. They are standing even today and are witness to history. If we could emerge strong and the best again and again at that time and with subsequent generations of rulers, it was because we shifted and changed in no time our tricks, methods, strategies and removed our mistakes and shortcomings fast. Whatever appeared unstable in *Satyug* was treated as prohibited in our period. Whatever changes were considered desirable in *Smritis* those changes were effected. Whatever had gone wrong was set right and thus we survived. The *Kshatriyas* in the battle fire, and the *Brahmins* in the *yajna* fire of *shuddhikaran* burnt Yavans, Shaks and Huns, reduced them to ashes, took them in our stomach-fold that in the whole *Bharat Varsha* no trace (not even name) of Greeks, *Huns* and *Shaks* was left. Then Muslims came up, came on the horizon. They reduced Syria, Iran, Babylonia and Africa to nothing. We proved small before their victorious trend. It was a huge and vast tumult, almost a deluge. We grappled with them for the last six hundred years and did not lose heart or spirit. We did not die. In the end, we developed sufficient resources, material and strength in ourselves. We learnt their tricks and strategies, and the use of their weapons. We snatched their weapons, and we arose, Hindus woke up. From the time of Mohammed Quasim to 1627, wherever Hindus fought with the Muslims, their defeat was certain, but from 1627 to 1795 wherever Muslims came to fight with Hindus, the Hindus trounced them. Therefore, we survived, and we survived by being victorious. We survived because we could face and tackle situations. To the extent it is true of the past, to that extent it is also true that we shall stick to our guns to face the present situation also. It will not happen like this: Since we have survived upto this day, we shall survive even now without doing anything."

"Today we have science in front of us. So whatever orthodoxies, conduct, *shastras* etc. come and prove true on the touchstone of science is our Hindu *dharma* today. Whatever is cheap, unstable burn it to ashes, because that is the *adharma* (undesirable element) of today, and is something that should be shunned at all costs. It is our good fortune that I see the natural strength of Hindu nation again surging up. If we fought with a little patience, using scientific means and fighting scientifically, I am sure we shall successfully fight out the battle started in crisis. We shall win as Hindus. When dying becomes unavoidable, we will die either like a warrior facing and fighting or like Guru Govind Singh. But we shall not die like a coward, by changing from Hindus to *Ahindus*. Never."

**Akhand Hindustan (United India)**

Veer Savarkar was totally opposed to the idea of creation of Pakistan. He had strongly opposed this demand. He was a supporter of *Akhand Hindu Rashtra*. He considered the Muslims demanding Pakistan as traitors. Opposing the Congress policy of appeasement of Muslims he fully expressed his ideas in this regard in an article entitled '*Akhand Hindustan Ya Pakistan*'. Some important extracts from that article are being given here below:

". . . Pandit Nehru, the loud speaker of Muslims, has been lecturing to Indian public for the last few days and is expressing his opposition to the creation of a Hindu State with great anger in stead of focusing light on plans of making India a Pakistan and taking India into confidence.

"It seems that the very demand of a Hindu state is a danger to his government. And that too such a danger that it appears to be more dangerous than the creation of a Muslim state in the neighbourhood, to which he should devote his mind at the earliest. In Pakistan, the bigot public from a religious point of view is still busy in murder, loot, arson and bloodshed and there every day thousands of persons come out on the streets shouting slogans, '*Hans ke liya hai Pakistan, Mar ke lenge Hindustan*' (We have got Pakistan happily and smiling. We will take India by beating and killing).

"Pandit Nehru and his half-nationalist companions, on one hand, are bearing the above threats and activities of Muslims against the Indian union with lost faces, and, on the other hand, displaying their oratorical bravery against the Hindus and saying that they would fight a bitter battle with those who want to establish a Hindu nation.

"Pandit Nehru says that if the organizers of Hindus tried to establish a Hindu state, they will meet the fate of Hitler and Mussolini. But Pandit Nehru forgets that the organizers of Hindus have amongst them hundreds of those commanders who fought in the first rank of India's fight for freedom at that time, when from a political point of view Gandhiji and Pandit Nehru were not even born."

"These half-nationalists say that the demand of a Hindu state is communal, mischievous, orthodax and goes against the progress of mankind. But these people, very conveniently refuse to say, before abusing the Hindu state, what precisely they mean by Hindu state. . . If the demand for a Hindu state is condemnable for the above reasons, then may I ask them: was not the demand for a Muslim state equally condemnable for the above reasons? Did the Muslims not demand Pakistani provinces on the basis that the Muslims had a majority in those provinces? Why did you accept that communal demand, and why did you divide our motherland into two parts for the establishment of an independent Muslim state?

". . . you say that our country cannot be called 'Hindustan' or 'Hindu nation' because it has many non-Hindu citizens also, but why do you and Gandhiji salute the new Muslim state by the name of Pakistan, which means a holy Muslim country, and it has a minority population of Hindus, Parsees, Christians etc. the non-Muslims? Is it not true that according to the interpretation of criterion of name offered by the United Nations the name of a country should be the name of the majority population in that country. Has your soul ever revolted when you pronounced Baluchistan, Waziristan, Afghanistan, Turkistan etc. when these countries have non-Muslim minorities also? Why does your breathing rhythm get disturbed when the name of 'Hindustan' or 'Hindu state' is mentioned to you as if a snake has bitten you?

"I want to clearly warn a thousandth time again the Hindu population that so long as they do not remove these half nationalist from administrative power, till then the Gandhiite Indianness will continue to provide the Muslims here opportunities to grab the prominent posts in police, army and other departments of the state. When the Pakistani forces attack India from north, west, east and south then these Muslims will immediately join them and then our Gandhiite government will step back, taken by surprise 'without prior notice' as has always happened, and Hindustan will be converted into '*Akhand Pakistan*'.

**Mohammed Panthi Hindu—An Illusory Concept**

A devotee of Pilkhua Ram Sharan Das, demonstrating his foolish idealism, wrote an article in 1962. According to this article, like so many *panths* (sects) in Hindu society, such as *Sanatani* Hindus, *Aryasamaji* Hindus, *Nanak panthi* Hindus, it would not be irrelevant to call Muslims as *Mohammed panthi* Hindus. Criticising the ideas in this article Veer Savarkar wrote:

"Religions such as Arya Samaj, Kabir Panth, Sikhism, Buddhism, etc. were born in India. Their founders were Hindus. Their holy land, and their places of holy pilgriomage are in India so they are born Hindus. But the Muslim religion and its founder Mohammed, and Christian religion and its founder Jesus Christs were born in foreign countries. Their holy land Mecca and Medina is in Arabia and not in India. So how can those people be called Hindus, whose holy land is not in India? It is a total illusion to call a person a '*Mohammed panthi*' Hindu who hates Kashi, Mathura and Ayodhya and considers Mecca and Medina as his place of pilgrimage."

### Religious Conversion ie Conversion of Nationality

Religious conversion of Hindus was considered as dangerous for the nation by Veer Savarkar. He was clearly of the opinion that if a Hindu converts his religion and becomes a Muslim or a Christian, then he would not consider India as his place of birth; his faith is changed to western nations. So India will remain India as long as Hindus retain their majority status. If India develops a majority of the followers of some other religion, then it will not be India:

". . . Change of religion means change of nationality. Hindus have developed toleration to the stage of excessive madness. . . . Hindu is prepared to lay down his life, his every thing for India only so long as he continues to be a Hindu. He can think of attaining salvation and heaven by laying down his life for his dear motherland, the most holy land. But if after changing his religion, he became a Muslim or a Christian, then why will he lay down his life for the pile of this soil? His holy land will change from Kashi to Medina. Therefore, you should understand for certain that the honest national, real devotee of India will be a Hindu only.

### Pay Him in the Same Coin—Right Policy

Veer Savarkar considered Gandhian non-violence as a blow for the future of Indian nation. He was of the opinion that a bully must be faced squarely and with steadfastness. Cautioning the Hindus against the principle of non-violence, he said:

"The root of Gandhian thinking is excessive non-violence. But according to my mind excessive violence is a monstrous crime. It can not be practised. It is fine to behave decently with decent people. To face an aggressor and give him a befitting reply through weapons is not considered a sin in Hindu culture. Rather it is an act of piety. Gandhiites say, 'We will neither be envious of anyone nor attack anyone. When we do not harbour jealousy against somebody, where is the need to attack him? Such ideas show only illusion and cowardice. It is possible that you would not be jealous, but who can guarantee that others would not be jealous of you. . . . Arm yourself, take weapons, and finish off the wicked. Kill the perpetrators of atrocities without giving a second thought, this has been ordained in the *Vedas*. This is our *dharma*."

**Great and Aggressive Military Power Necessary**

Veer Savarkar considered great and aggressive military power necessary for the defence of the nation and its all-round development. He expressed his ideas in this regard through articles and speeches on a number of occasions.

In 1958, during the end ceremony of 'Abhinav Bharat', in his speech he said:

"For the defence of great Indian state and its growth and development the foremost among all requirements is great military strength, because mankind today on political level is standing on the basis of nation and armed strength. Only those countries are really independent whose independence is backed by strong nationalism and armed strength, and are trying to make an impact on other strong nations. If you want to survive in the present day situation and the horse-race of aggressive nations, you should better give up your shortsightedness and illusion of non-violence and talking peace, and immediately undertake the work of making India a Hindu nation, the most powerful country armed with the latest weapons. .. . . We cannot be called big in comparison with the big nations which are armed with the latest weapons, until we are also armed with the latest weapons like them. Talking of neutrality glibly without strong armed strength is meaningless. Only that country's desire for peace is relevant which is armed with strength and weapons. Therefore, the rulers of states today should take up on a vast scale the work of making their armed forces strong with latest weapons in the interest of defence. As in other countries, the youths and adults in India should compulsorily be trained in the latest and chivalrous weapons and education. In fact, the developed young generation of

India, in the interest of the defence of our nation, should be so combat-efficient that within a span of five years at least one crore Hindu youths, armed with the latest weapons in Navy, Army and Air Force, are always prepared to safeguard our borders on all four sides."

Before the 1961 Chinese aggression also, Veer Savarkar said in a statement that we should be aggressive, as only then the defence of the nation is possible.

"I am worried. We have got independence, no doubt. But what will its future be? Who will defend this country and how? How will the eunuch-like and dejected faced Congress leaders discharge this duty? China was attacking on Indian borders, did Pandit Nehru not know this? China developed 400-mile-long roads and built steel bridges—did the Intelligence Department of the Administration not know this? But just due to fear they did not make even a mention of it. Had we adopted an aggressive posture, we would never have faced this problem? Had we, immediately after independence, clearly demarcated our borders and by entering into 'No man's land' declared it as 'Hindu Man's Land', then this disaster would just not have occurred."

In fact, the downfall of a nation is due to its own people in power. If they are hard working, honest and competent, then this question would not crop up that the nation is not progressing. In the opinion of Veer Savarkar, a weak ruler can never look after the interests of the nation. In an article in 1961, he wrote:

"I have the least of intentions to be the President of the nation. But imagine, if I somehow gain power, then within two years I'll show that India is stronger than Russia under the presidentship of Khrushchev. I'll increase the strength of the army with the latest training and weapons; and if the situation so desired, as in the case of Khrushchev in United Nations when he took his shoe in his hand and challenged, exactly in the same manner I'll take my book in my hand and challenge the enemy country. The impact of a country depends on the armed powers of its soldiers. The impact of Khrushchev is due to his atomic weapons."

The breach of faith which China resorted to vis-a-vis India due to the latter's policy of non-violence was commented upon in 1961 by Veer Savarkar when, in the course of a speech, he said:

". . . Our policies and strength are not steady and effective. See, that China which could not liberate Formosa, which could not take a small island named Macao from Portugal, that same China usurps thousands of miles of *Bharat Varsha*. This incident has only one meaning—Our power has not created any impact on him, any fear in his heart. Who will be afraid of and why, of a country, which declares, "We shall not fight under any circumstances, 'Our reply to bullets will be our letters of protest'?"

Compulsory military training, huge armed forces, and the manufacture of weapons makes any small nation strong. Israel is the concrete example of it. In the 26th January, 1954 issue of *Kesari* published from Poona, Veer Savarkar, expressing his ideas on the subject, wrote:

"It is very relevant to take into consideration the example of Israel. This nation was so completely and in such a manner uprooted and thrown away that not a trace of it was to be seen anywhere. But it is reborn after hundreds of years, and in the presence of those Arabs who were completely armed and who had surrounded it. But the first thing which this nation did was the compulsory military training to all able bodied men and women. It put ordnance factories for the manufacture of latest weapons. It entered into military treaties and agreements with powerful nations, and in this manner made itself so strong that all those enemy nations which had surrounded it could not dare attack it even with their combined strength. Not only this. Now that small Israel from time to time intrudes into the borders of Arab countries and gives them a hell of time. Now we should try to increase our military strength, otherwise China and Pakistan will some day openly attack us and we will come to a sorry pass. On that day it would not be possible to face the aggressor with the spirit of world peace and *Panch-Sheel*, and only that country will win who has greater armed strength".

On 15th January, 1961 when in Poona, Veer Savarkar's *Mritunjaya* ceremony was going on, he, in the course of his speech, strongly said that the Government of India should not lag behind in the manufacture of atomic weapons:

"I want that our army is the most modern in the world and is armed with the latest weapons. I go to the extent of saying that we should have atomic and nuclear weapons in our hands. I would go even one more step ahead and call upon our scientists that they should invent the most lethal weapons, even hydrogen bomb. We want all this for our army—all these most modern and the latest weapons. Our generation should put this objective before itself. Our youths should make themselves the latest. They should join Army, Navy and Air Force. In Europe, every healthy youth is imparted military training. He has to undergo compulsory military training. Therefore, my young friends! It should be your only, and highest duty to take military training. Join A.C.C., N.C.C. or Territorial Army. . . when I refer to Pandit Nehru, I do not mean him as a person, but I refer to rulers. The purpose of my saying is that we should create an atmosphere of war in the country once. Once that is done, then I am sure that it is the citizens who will ask the government to talk tough and act tough, even if the government is weak and lacks courage. Then this staggering democracy of ours will not fall on the ground or be defeated in a moment. Therefore, always remember, democracy may be most ideal form of government in the world, but if it lacks armed strength in its backyard, then it is not safe."

# Six Important Speeches

The speeches of Veer Savarkar in Ahmedabad, Nagpur, Calcutta, Mathura, Bhagalpur and Kanpur sessions of Hindu Mahasabha offer a good introduction to his philosophy of life. Though in these speeches also he has expressed his ideas on Hindu, *Hindutva*, Hindu Nation and *Akhand Bharat* yet they have a special significance in understanding his philosophy of life. So these speeches are being presented here in abridged form:

**Ahmedabad Session—1937**

In this speech Veer Savarkar has expressed his ideas on integrity and unity of India, interpretation of the word 'Hindu' and 'Hindu himself is a nation'.

**India Should Remain Undivided**

If for the moment we keep apart the artificial provincial division of India caused by political rape and forced upon us at present, then one thing will become clear to all of us that all of us are bound by the strong, indivisible and stable bonds of blood, religion and country. Whatever the consequences, taking this as our objective we should declare that the India of tomorrow is one and undivided and should remain so from Kashmir to Rameshwaram and from Sindhu to Assam not (only) because it is joint, but because it forms one inalienable nation.

**Interpretation of the Word 'Hindu'**

The outward form of the fixed and authorized action of Hindu Mahasabha depends upon exact interpretation of the word 'Hindu'. So, we should first of all clear the interpretation of *Hindutva* itself. When on the clarification of interpretation and prevalence of this word, it is properly understood and assimilated, then alone various doubts rising in our own people will be set at rest, and we will be able to silence effectively our opponents by giving them a cutting reply, who are raising and spreading various objections and illusions against us in society. It is our extremely good fortune that we have got a definite interpretation of the word 'Hindu' with us, though we might have been compelled to go through a dense jungle of search to arrive at it. . . The explanation of the word 'Hindu' is like this :

आसिन्धु सिन्धु पर्यन्ता यस्य भारत भूमिका।
पितृभूः पुण्य भूश्चैव स वै हिन्दुरिति स्मृतः॥

*(Asindhu sindhu paryanta yasya bharat bhumika*
*Pitribhuh punyabhushchaiva sa vai hinduriti smritah)*

i.e., any person who considers this *bharat bhumi*, spread from Sindhu to the ocean, as his *pitribhumi* (fatherland) and *punya bhumi* (holy land) and says so in an anthentic way, every such person is a 'Hindu'.

I have to clarify one thing here that the followers of some other religions which were not born in *Bharat Varsha* would be unrelated and would not be called 'Hindus'. The reason is that religion is only one part or characteristic of *Hindutva*. But if we have an internal and serious desire that our above definition is not proved doubtful or wrong, then what we require is that, staying within the ambit of *Hindutva* we observe the other and important parts also equally seriously. In order that a man calls himself a 'Hindu' it would not be sufficient for him to say that he followed a religion which was born in India, i.e. he considered India his holy land. This is also necessary for him to be a 'Hindu' that he considers this country as his fatherland. For my speech today it is not the occasion to offer a detailed and comprehensive explanation. Therefore, I would refer to my book *Hindutva* for detailed information on this matter. In this book I have quoted and mentioned all requirements in a logical manner and provided detailed and extensive thought on the matter. It would be sufficient to say in the present context that the entire Hindu world is bound not only by the bonds of religion (i.e. not by the bond of holy land where he and his religion were born) but also by one culture, one language, one history, and (more important than this) by an automatic bond of his fatherland, and from these bonds he is a self-proved nation and an authentic independent society. . ."

**Hindu a Nation in Itself**

". . . (I never thought) you will ask me this question also— since there is so much of gap, interval in every small thing, how can we address Hindus as a nation? To such people my reply is that there is no country on the face of this earth which has total unity and oneness of language, culture, ancestry and religion. No public of a country is authorised to be called by the name of a nation by its unity of living together and lack of untold differences *than by its clear differences of forms* expressed in living together. People, who object to or find fault with calling Hindus a nation, are the ones who accept the residents of Great Britain, United States, Russia, Germany and other countries as a nation. I want to ask such persons what is their criterion of calling these countries nations? . . . With this situation obtaining, when you people call them a nation on the basis of a common country, language, culture and holy land, then the Hindus also qualify for being a nation. They have lived together on a land for ages and got into a harmony of living. For them *Hindustan* is clearly their inalienable fatherland. In this have grown all their languages which have developed and perfected day after day and their ancient *dharma-shastras* and the sayings (*suktis*) of their ancestors are collected in a holy form in those languages and earned glory all around. In whose case the genes of Manu have descended to this day through marriages maintaining purity of blood and crossbreeding for better progeny. Their social functions and other initiations and processes have no less commonality than those of the people in England. *Vedic Rishis* are a common subject to them, for journey into the last and divine knowledge. Panini and Patanjali are their grammarians. . . In fact, barring mutual exclusiveness of Hindu society, if we look at it from the point of view of an independent, vast and general society, then this ground level appears separate from any other general society in a clear and high proportion. One country, one ancestry, one religion, one language—if you test any society on any one of these criteria for the qualification of nation, then Hindu race explicitly appears an authentic claimant for nationhood on all these criteria."

### The Meaning of '*Hindustan Ka Swarajya*'

Clarifying the meaning of the freedom or *swarajya* (self-rule) of Hindustan, Veer Savarkar in this speech said that its real meaning is 'an independent nation for Hindus with political rights, and their allround development.'

"In common parlance the meaning of the word '*swarajya*' is the political freedom of this land, the freedom of the geographical area known by the name of Hindustan. But now the time has come when we separate the above sentences and expressions and understand the meanings hidden deep inside them. Any country or a geographical area does not become a nation by itself. Our country is a place where we live with our relatives, friends and the persons of our caste, our near and dear ones. We love it for that reason, and in a figurative language from that point of view, we express it in words such as 'our national existence'. i.e. the freedom of Hindustan would mean the freedom of our people, our caste and our nation. Therefore, when we use the word '*Hindi Swarajya*' or '*Hindi Swadhinata*' then it would mean, to the extent it is connected with Hindu nation, the political freedom of Hindus, a freedom which enables Hindus to develop themselves to the highest possible level."

### Anti-national Muslim Ideas

Regarding the ideas of Muslim League at that time, Veer Savarkar, in this speech, expressed himself in the following words:

"You should call it the good fortune of Hindu community that this year in the meeting of Muslim League in Lucknow, Mr. Jinnah and other Muslim leaders deliberately expressed their inner objectives in more authentic, clear and patient way. I thank them for this. If we are together then it is better to have an enemy who comes out openly than a friend whose credentials are doubtful. . . Now it would be enough for us to refer to the speeches and resolutions of the Lucknow meeting only to clearly demonstrate the anti-Hindu, anti-Hindi and foreign activities of Muslims. It is not required to do any more things than this exposure now. They desire that pure Urdu should occupy the post of national language of Hindi state. As a mother tongue it is not spoken by more than two crore Muslims. If we count Muslims also among them, twenty crore people do not understand and follow it. On the other hand is Hindi which is called mother tongue by seven crore people, and besides it, more than ten crore people can understand it. Therefore, it has many more literary qualities as well. . . In respect to national script as well, their similar insistence continues and they want Urdu as national script. However important, they do not have any duty towards *nagri* script. . . Even then the Muslims consider Urdu their cultural heritage. You this characteristic only they insists that Urdu should be the national language and Urdu script should be the national script, and Muslims should accordingly get that high status. Therefore, the Hindus and other non-Muslim communities living in *Bharat Varsha* should go to hell. These days Muslims find it difficult even to suffer the recital of national song '*Vande Matarma*'. Poor Hindus who uselessly worry for unity; they made post-haste efforts to prune it short, to make it low in stature . . . This problem can not be solved till a pure Urdu song composed by Iqbal or Jinnah himself, treating India as Pakistan or a land dedicated to Muslim State and singing paeans to it, is accepted as national anthem."

**Muslims—An Obstacle in Unity**

". . . The threats which the Muslims are giving to Hindus with regard to consequences mean only this that if their anti-national and other demands, mad in nature, are not accepted, then they will not join hands with Hindus in their fight for freedom. It is required of Hindus that they give a clear and categorical reply to Muslims, saying that we needed only this kind of friendship. And we need it even today and that we shall create a Hindi state in which, irrespective of caste, creed, ancestry or religion, all citizens will be treated on the basis of 'One man one vote'. Though we are a majority in this country, we do not demand any special privileges for Hindu community. . . They should understand well that we know all their tricks. Recently the Muslim nations from Arabistan to Afghanistan have formed a line of aggressive alliances and started an anti-Hindu movement under the garb of "all Islamisation", and is inspired by religious and cultural hatred. A cruel tendency to strongly suppress and smash Hindus is found among Muslims of frontier area. We have understood it all very well, and will not give a blank cheque by trusting you. We are committed and prepared to win *swarajya* for ourselves in a manner in which our 'self' is safe along with the 'self' of all other parts of India. We did not prepare ourselves to grapple with England with an intention to replace one master with another. But with an intention and purpose that in our home we ourselves are the masters. This is the aim of Hindus. . . Side by side when they understand that they cannot live without the assistance and goodwill of the Hindus, they themselves will be ready with a demand for unity, and that too, not for doing some good to Hindus, but for their own welfare. The Hindu-Muslim unity which is established in this manner will be a valuable and important unity. It is after paying a heavy price that Hindus have realized that to strive for unity is an effort for losing it only. In future the guiding principle with Hindus, in respect of Hindu-Muslim unity, will be only this: If you come, you are welcome. If you do not come, then without you; and if you oppose us then with whatever we can do to counter you, we shall move ahead, the Hindu nation will definitely make its own future."

**Regarding Other Minorities**

Expressing his ideas regarding other minorities, in addition to Muslims, Veer Savarkar in this speech stated:

"Other minority communities of India are not going to pose any problems in the activity of strengthening Hindi nation. Parsees have fought along with Hindus shoulder to shoulder in their fight against the British colonialism. They are not religious bigots or perverse people. Right from *Mahatma* Dada Bhai Nauroji to the famous revolutionary lady, Madame Bhikaji Cama, Parsees have joined hands with Hindi patriots. This Hindu nation, whom they considered the source of salvation of their clan, has always received their goodwill prior to their expression of any other thought. From cultural point of view also they are our nearest and dearest ones known. The same thing in some measure can be said about Hindi Christians. Though they have participated little in the national struggles mooted by us, they have at least not conducted themselves in a manner which may be burdensome or problem to us. They are a bit less in religious bigotry and bow their heads to political reasoning. Otherwise, too, they are a very small minority and do not oppose our national aspirations. All this makes one thing certain that all these minority brethren will prove to be trustworthy citizens inspired by national pride. . . With regard to Anglo-Indian community this much is clear that the present obduracy and the lion share available to them in the form of Reform Act will disappear in no time with the withdrawal of England from Indian scene. Their in-born political sharpness will soon bring them in line with others. Even if this does not happen, it would be possible to bring them on the right track."

In the end of this speech Veer Savarkar, forecasting the end of the British rule and India attaining independence, said:

"Who knows? It is possible that after some time in future, if not in this generation, then in the next generation of our children, some more lucky president of Hindu Mahasabha, standing on this very place, will break the news of success in a loud voice and say: What happened to the Huns, the Greek and the Shak aggressors in the past, in the same manner no trace of the British pelf and power is left in India today. The flag of Hindu community is flying aloft the high ranges of the Himalayas, Hindustan has become independent and the Hindu community has become fortunate again."

**Nagpur Session—1938**

In his speech in this session, taking a bird's eye-view of Indian history, Veer Savarkar focused light on the gradual development of Hindu nation, its rise, the communal tendency of Muslims and the future programmes of the nation.

### Hindu Nation—Not a Paper Treaty

"It must have become clear by now that at least for the last five thousands of years our ancestors, from the Vedic period itself, were busy in making a Hindu nation by organizing the people of this country in their religious, communal, cultural and political elements, which is spread all over *Bharat* by the name of Hindu nation and all people consider *Bharat* as their fatherland and holy land. Barring China, no other country of the world can claim of continued national integration for such a long period as India which has grown as an integrated Hindu nation. The development of Hindu nation did not take place as a mushroom. Hindu nation has not been constituted through a treaty—it has not been made by a piece of paper. The nation was not made for sitting silently. This is not a nation forged out of foreigners. It has grown on this land, and its roots are spread far and wide. It has not been imagined to tease Muslims or any other person in the world. On the other hand it is a solid reality like the Himalayas. . . ."

### The Order of Rise of Hindu Nation

We have told you the history of the growth and development of the living elements of Hindu nation upto the fall of Maratha empire, i.e. upto 1818. Later on, after the fall of Maratha empire, the British empire arrived in India. After the fall of the state of Sikh Hindus in Punjab, the Britishers got an opportunity to establish their authority unhindered all over the country. The Britishers saw that all the battles that they had to fight to conquer India were fought with Hindu kings. Therefore, the first worry of the Britishers was how to destroy the Hindu nation. The Englishmen first offered political patronage to Christian bishops to convert Hindus to Christianity. But the mutiny of 1857 opened their eyes. . . after this they thought out another policy to destroy Hindu nation from its roots. They began imparting western education to Hindu youths, which aimed at destroying nationality. The first batch of Hindu youths who received Western education with great eagerness was completely divorced of ancient *Hinduness* and the spirit of *Hindutva*. They had no knowledge of Hindu religion, Hindu culture, and Hindu history. Contrary to it, Muslims were way behind in Western education. Consequently their communal steadfastness could not be destroyed. The British government was happy over it. They knew that in the Indian context if anything could challenge their political sovereignty it could be the national awakening of the Hindus and the spirit of establishing *Hindu pad Padshahi* in Bharat. . ."

**Provincial Unity Not Compulsory for Nation**

"The congress has been trying to merge Muslims in India for the last fifty years, but it has failed. Why? What are its main reasons? Is it asking them, first be Indian, and then a Muslim? It is not that the Muslims do not want an Indian nation, but their concept of national unity of India is not based on provincial unity. If any Muslim has expressed these sentiments of his heart, then it is the leader of Mopla rebellion, Ali Musaliyar. In battle he converted by force thousands of Hindu men, women and children to Islam, and those who refused this religious conversion were put to sword. Justifying his activities in this regard he said, "The permanent unity between Hindus and Muslims can be effected only in one way and that is that all Hindus are converted to Islam. The Hindus who refuse it are the enemies of Hindu-Muslim unity. They are, therefore, traitors and deserve to be slain." The words were uttered by Ali Musaliar in his mother tongue without any adulteration. Clarifiers like Mohammed Ali will say the same thing in such a round-about manner that nobody can understand it. But it boils down to this. We do not require provincial unity for the creation of a nation, we need religious, cultural and communal unity. Indian National Congress could not comprehend this element and this is the reason why it failed in its objective.

**Religions Bigotry of Indian Muslims**

"This is the biggest question and the Congressi Hindus

do not consider this matter even for a minute at the beginning of the Congress session. Nor do they consider it at that time when the session of the Congress is suspended to enable Muslims to offer *namaz*. It is useless to declare only the Muslim League as communal. It is not a news, it is a reality that the entire Muslim community is imbued in the spirit of communalism and this includes Congressi Muslims also. We should try to understand why they are communal? The Congressi Hindus do not want to think about it, primarily. They fear that if they considered this question then they would be obliged to give up their insistence on provincial unity as religious bigotry or foolishness. You may call it religious bigotry or foolishness. But it is a solid reality for Muslims. You cannot win by abusing them. You will have to face it in the situation in which it is. In the background of the reasons I have stated above, it is completely humanly justified for Muslims that they express their indifference to provincial nationality. The Congressmen know it. It appears that the Congressmen are completely ignorant of the history of Muslims, their knowledge of elements and their political tendencies. . . . The Muslim League has openly declared that India will be divided into two parts, one Muslim Federation, and the other Hindu Federation. The British government is trusting its loving wife so much to spite the Hindus, just consider it well and deeply. It is possible that the British government itself is spited in the process. Whatever the case, it is the task before the British government and not before us. The British government should be worried about it. In reality, the only work of Hindus is to determine that we would be slaves neither to the British government, nor to Muslims. We would ourselves be masters in our own home, in the land of Hindus, Hindustan."

### First Duty of Hindu Organisers

". . . Indian Muslims never co-operate in a common way, at a common level in forging unity at provincial stage. Therefore, it is the duty of we organisers of Hindus that we correct our first mistake. The first political crime our Congressi Hindus committed under ignorance and with which they are continuing even today is the chasing of mirage of provincial nationality, and in this pointless race they want to kill that living Hindu nation which was nourished with great love and care. . . they are the masters of it. If you call it Indian nation then it is to be considered a synonym of Hindu nation only. For us, Hindus, Bharat and Hindustan are one and the same country. We are Indians also by being Hindu, and Hindu also by being Indian."

"I am sure you all agree with this Hindu policy, but all of you must be confronted with a question particularly, as to how it will take place. How will this policy be put to practise? This Hindu organization is in a weak state; it faces many problems; how shall that powerful situation be realised? There is only one reply: Please do not lose hope. We have a very powerful weapon close by. Spread your hand in the right direction and seize the weapon. It begins here."

**Boycott Congress**

Calling the people to boycott Congress in elections, he said:

"Vote only for Hindu nationalists, and do not cast your vote in favour of Congress candidates, because these Congress-men consider it inglorious to call themselves Hindus, but since according to constitution every candidate had to declare his caste and religion, these Congress candidates at that time forgetting their nationality quietly write down their caste, religion etc., and ask their casteists to vote for them so that they win by more votes. But once elected, they consider it an insult to be called as Hindus.

"But if you clearly tell them that you are not going to vote to such two-faced Hindus, then 75% of the nationalists will take oath of the pledge-letter of Hindu Mahasabha, but will not like to lose the opportunity of being elected a member of Central Assembly or becoming a minister."

**The Requirement of a Hindu Nationalist Party**

In this context, focusing light on the importance of a nationalist party following solid Hindu thinking Veer Savarkar said,

"All the followers of Hindu organizations like Sanatanis Arya Samajis, saints and sages should decide that they are not going to vote for Congress candidates; then in the coming elections Hindu Mahasabha will come in majority. If this is not possible, and you are elected in a minority, stop the government acting in an arbitrary manner. If this happens, then the whole scene will change. A Hindu nation will rise in the country and every Hindu will walk with his chest erect.

"Therefore, Ye organizers of Hindus! From today you start voting for Hindu nationalists and you will see that complaints evaporate like smoke. When you achieve this, then one day you shall see the emergence of an independent, powerful Hindu nation, in which all those citizens have common rights, who are true Indian citizens. There are political seats of power. Attain them, get them. Raise the flag of Hindu nation, and see to it that Bharat remains always Hindustan. It does not turn into a Pakistan or Englishtan."

**Calcutta Session—1939**

In this session the main topics of Veer Savarkar's speech were communal riots, Hyderabad Agitation and *Rashtra-Bhasha*.

**The Panic of Communal Riots**

"Muslims have played a bloody Holi with the blood of Hindus in Sindh province, Sakkhar, and other places. In North West Frontier Provice, the border Pathans have created a panic among Hindus by constantly attacking and killing them and looting their property. At many places in United Provinces, Bengal and Bihar bigot Muslims have carried out anti-Hindu riots and perpetrated atrocities on them. And the agreement between the government and Congress-Muslim League will turn out to be more harmful than the one famous with the name of 'Communal Agreement'; and beyond it all is the World War II which offered the government an opportunity to take the constitutional progress of India back by fifty years and to act again in the old arbitrary manner which continued upto this day in some form or the other. There are a few problems which must be considered in depth and detail."

### Satyagraha Movement against the Nizam, Hyderabad

The successful movement of the Hindus against the atrocities of the Nizam, Hyderabad, was termed *Dharma Yuddha* by Veer Savarkar. He said,

"Among all the incidents of this year from the point of view of Hindu organisation and from the stand point of indication to our future programmes and policies, the most important is the *satyagraha* in hyderabad, which we carried out for six months against the anti-Hindu policies of the Nizam government. In reality, it was a religions war (*dharma-yuddha*). It was religious on one hand, and equally courageous on the other. Our Arya Samaji brethren bore the heat of this war. More than ten thousand Arya brethren participated in it, and fought so courageously that they showed that the fire of *yojna*, lit by *Maharshi* Dayanand, the organizer of the best Hindu organization, was increasing day by day and the purpose of his life has not fallen into incompetent hands. In addition to this the demands, which the organizers of Hindu organizations, put before the Nizam government, it had to accept under compulsion, and in my opinion this one can be counted among our achievements. In respect of Hindu objective, this *dharma-yuddha* has proved one thing that in spite of various differences and opinions of caste among Hindus, Hindutva is still coursing through our veins in an extensive nationalistic spirit."

### Shiva Temple of Delhi

The entire *Bharat Varsha* should offer its tributes for its tributes for the unique way in which Hindus have carried out their *satyagraha* for Shiva Temple of Delhi. From this also we receive the same warning that in anti-Hindu attacks the Congress does not defend Hindu interests. It will not defend in future either. In fact, it cannot defend them. But all these pains and sacrifices for Shiva Temple of Delhi will not go waste, if the Hindu voters of Delhi send such Hindus of Hindu organizations to represent them, who have not become the slaves of Congress, and who pledge to safeguard

Hindu interests. The sincere spirit of Hindutva which this agitation has thrown up will prove itself in the real Shiva form."

**Dev-Dhasha, Rashtra-Bhasha and Rashtra-Lipi**

Here light has been focused an Sanskrit language, a symbol of India's unity, national language Hindi and the national script *Dev-nagari* in terms of their significance, specific virtues and suitability and their scientific character.

"Sanskritised Hindi, formed and nourished from Sanskrit language, shall be our national language. Sanskrit language, besides being the most ancient among all the languages in the most perfected and enriched language. In addition to it, it is the most pious language for us, Hindus. Our religious scriptures, history, deep spiritual knowledge and culture—all these are so deeply related to and inherent in Sanskrit that it is really the head of our Hindu race. It is the mother of most of our mother tongues. It has fed them from its breasts. All the languages of Hindus, whether emanating from Sanskrit or formed with amalgamation with it, can grow and be prosperous only when they are nourished by Sanskrit. Therefore, Sanskrit should necessarily form a part of the curriculum of ancient languages to be learnt by a Hindu youth.

"Here it would be interesting to tell you how two ex-presidents of the Congress tried to solve the problem of national language and national script. Maulana Abul Kalam Azad says that the national language *Hindustani* should be like Urdu. Pandit Jawahar Lal Nehru goes a step ahead and says that the national language should be either of Aligarh school or of Osmania University. That would be most appropriate for 28 crore Hindus. Subhash Babu, the glory of India, scores a point over his predecessor Jawahar Lal Nehru in wisdom. He says that the most appropriate script for India would be the Roman script. This is how the Congress thinking ponders over national issues. How practical can it be, the less said, the better. Your *Vasumati, Anant Bazar Patrika* and all other Bengali papers would not be published in Roman script. 'Vande Mataram' would now in this new script be written something like this:

*'Tomaro pratima ghadibe mandire mandire'*

( तोमार प्रतिमा गड़िबे मन्दिरे मन्दिरे )

And see in what a fine form the *Geeta* would be written:

*'dharmakshetre kurukshitre' samveta yuyutsavah'*

( धर्मक्षेत्रे कुरुक्षेत्रे समवेता युयुत्सव: )

It will be like this:

We Hindus should ask the people of Europe and Arabia accept *nagri* script and Hindi language. This proposal of ours should not be considered impracticable by those dogged and optimist persons who imagine Urdu to be the national language and think that Marathas will read Urdu and the *Vedas* in the *Gurukuls* of Arya Samaj will be taught in Roman script.

**Anti-Hindu Congress Government**

The provincial governments of Congress interfered in the religious activities of Hindus, due to its appeasement policy towards Muslims. Criticising this, Veer Savarkar said in his speech,

". . . In Barabanki Hindus have been stopped from performing *Aratis* and blowing of conch in their temples. At many places the Hindus are prohibited from throwing colours on other Hindus. In Jaunpur the Magistrate was attacked by Muslims, but on the recommendation of the Secretary of the Muslim League, the accused were let off. The Congress government has given representation in services more than the proportion of their population. In United Provices the proportion of Muslim population is 14% but the Congress government there has, out of 4 collectors, appointed 3 Muslim collectors. Among 13 deputy collectors, 8 are Muslims. And like this at many other places. Every Hindu should read the memorandum published by the Congress government in United Provinces. It is a very competent memorandum, contradicting its own principles. The Congress government secretly sent this memorandum only to the Muslims, but some Hindu Mahasabhaites, who have been cursed as traitors could lay their hands on this 'national' *dharma-grantha* and they printed and distributed it."

### Future Programme

In the end Veer Savarkar, talking about removal of untouchability, military training etc. and future programmes, said,

"Until something extraordinary happens unexpectedly, an we are called upon to perform more of our duties, till then all the Hindu Mahasabhas, whether local or provincial, should make all possible efforts to do three things:

(1) Remove Untouchability

(2) Pressurise all schools, colleges and universities to make military training compulsory for students, and make your young men join Navy, Air Force and Army.

(3) As far as possible, prepare your voters that in elections they vote for the candidates of Hindu orgnaisations, who pledge to safeguard the interests of Hindus; and never vote for those Congressmen who cannot work with full freedom and courage for the protection of Hindu interests so long as they are bound by Congress discipline and Congress ticket."

### Madurai Session, 1940

In his speech in this session he exhorted Hindus to compulsorily practice the use of weapons. Besides this, he asked Hindus to oppose the demand for Pakistan, told them about the uselessness of *satyagraha.*

### Be Warriors and Industrialise

The attitude of Hindus towards war should be oriented towards making the community, soldiers and in accordance with the need for industrialization. If Hindus refuse to join the Army, Navy, Air Force and ordnance factories manufacturing war materials, its immediate repercussion would be that Muslims would sit on your chest, and in your dream of weakening the British government you will find that you have strengthened those who are in no way less than other and bent upon making you a slave in your own land. No League-Congress treaty without making Hindu Mahasabha agreeable to it, can barter or pawn Hindu rights."

### Well-Wisher a Friend

The opinion of Veer Savarkar, in this respect, was that one who is a well-wisher of our country, irrespective of his practice of any political system, is our friend. We should make the best of such friendship in the best interests of the country. He said,

"The demand of prominent Congress leaders such as Pandit Jawahar Lal Nehru that he (Savarkar) should shed more light on his war objectives appears useless. The reason is that Britain is under pressure and secondly shedding any light on these objectives would be futile if they are not practised. Britain could do this by making India free and giving it a democratic constitution, but it did nothing of this kind. History and politics tell us that no constitution or social system can be useful to all under all circumstances. As farm as the interests of Britain are concerned, it is harping upon personal freedom and democracy, and shows great love for it. But did it in one day, under conditions of war, abandoned its democratic ideas and constitution and voted in favour of solid dictatorship? . . . 'Fight Germans because they have a dictatorship there, and love the English men, the French and the Americans because they are democratic'. Saying so and demanding help from Indians does not have any meaning. A wise policy and practical politics demand that we should make friends with these who serve our national interests, it doe not matter which political philosophy they pursue, and we should maintain friendship with them so long as they are useful to us."

### Both: Not Serving One another, But One's Own Self

At the time of World War II Britain gave some concessions to Indians and Indian soldiers went to fight on behalf of Britain. In the opinion of Veer Savarkar, the purpose of these concessions was not serving the interests of Indians, but it was doing so in its own self-interest.

Along with this, he saw the help of Indian soldiers to Britain from a different point of view. In his opinion it was in the interest of Indians, as they gained the practice and experience of war.

Hindus should take advantage of war and make themselves busy in industrialization and militarization. We should take advantage of those concessions which it is giving under compulsion. At present we are getting some opportunities which we did not get in the last 50 years, and which we could not get in the next 50 years with demands and protests. Remember, the British government is not extending these concessions in our interest, but in its own interest. We are also not joining the war efforts to help Britain, but are doing so for our own advantage. We do not object to helping Britain if that helps us."

### *Satyagraha*, an Election Stunt

In this speech Veer Savarkar considered sloganeering, filling jails, *Satyagraha* etc. only an election stunt.

"A man who is afraid of being pressed by others is pressed by good conduct. Organisers of Hindus trust their political wisdom and are confident that they can defend themselves in all circumstances. Therefore, we should think as to what advantage can be derived from war situation; what steps can we take in our interest and support and to what extent we can further Hindu interests?"

". . . Shouting slogans and going to jail. Is it a game? It cannot be useful to the country. Yes, it can be called a stunt for the forthcoming election. Hindu Sabha is not prepared to do two things. If it finds that there is an advantage in *satyagraha*, it can start it. But it will be harmful to our interests at this juncture."

It is evident that though *stayagraha* was not completely prohibited, it was considered a useless activity. He emphasized military training in its place. He was clear in his views that the country could be liberated only through armed revolution. He said so at the end of his speech:

"Both a minister of India and the Viceroy have declared that India will be a part of Commonwealth after the war. We opposed the division of India and demanded that it should not be accepted. Mr. Emery has made it clear. Our demands in respect of armed forces, too, are going to be accepted. The government has accepted Hindu Mahasabha as a representative institution of Hindus. Now the British government is repeating only one thing that all the parties of India should come together and prepare their constitution. It does not take into account the minority or majority in this respects. We will fight on this issue at an appropriate time and force Britain to accept our demand. In brief, giving up the idea of *satyagraha*, we should take advantage of this opportunity and Hindus should join the efforts of increasing military power."

**Bhagalpur Session, 1941**

It would be proper to describe the Bhagalpur session a struggle, and not a session. It has been described earlier. In this struggle Savarkar was arrested, and he could not read out his speech. As a result, this speech was read by other persons. Veer Savarkar had focused on the following issues in this session:

**Regarding Ban**

Bihar government had banned this session. Therefore, he took this matter at the beginning of the speech.

"I hope that if the representatives of Hindu organizations from different parts of Hindustan would gather and keep themselves ready for jail, lathi-charge and other sacrifices, then this 23rd session of Mahasabha shall be the most successful. I think this speech will not be read in Bhagalpur. Besides, the time left is little. Therefore, I write a few things for the guidance of Hindu movement.

**Nepal King - Hope of Hindu Future**

In the heart of the devotee of *Hindutva*, Veer Savarkar, there is unlimited respect and faith for the only Hindu king in the world, the king of Nepal. He saw the Hindu state Nepal and the king there as the hope for the future of Hindus. He expressed his feelings in the following words:

"Nepal is the only Hindu state. It is the biggest

representative of the bright past of Hindus, and more that that it is a hope of the splendid Hindu future. Therefore, I express devotion to the *Maharaja* of Nepal on behalf of all Hindus. The elderly *Maharaja* Shamsher Jang Bahadur Rana realizes that the future of Nepal is tied with *Hindutva.* Hindu in reality is a national unit, and to change his destiny is in the hands of Nepal. I have learnt from some reliable sources that the number of mosques is increasing in Nepal, and in the adjoining areas boys and girls are coaxed into accepting Islam. The government of Nepal should not consider this difficulty of Hindus as a minor matter and be on talent. In the initial stage these mosques are said to be built as prayer houses, but later on they work as the hot bed for anti-Hindu orthodoxy."

**To Muslims**

Now the time has come for Muslims in India to face reality. It is in their interest that they stopped building castles in the air. They should realize that they are a minority and it has no meaning to say that they convert Hindu majority into a minority. The *shuddhi* movement and the awareness of their manliness among Hindus have brought the question of League in India to an end. Now if an Allanddin or an Aurangzeb is re-born even then it is not possible to debase a dozen Hindus by force or fraud. Thousands of Hindu fa nilies in many villages have been forcibly made Muslims. The Muslim *goondas* thought that villages would then join Pakistan for ever. But as soon as the intensity of dispute decreased, those debased Hindus are more strong'v opposed to Muslims than earlier. These things reveal tha Muslims will always be in a minority in India. Therefore, they should frame their political agenda keeping this reality in mind. Today, on the basis of their present population, they should not entertain any desire to get even one seat in Assembly or in government. If they are entertaining the hope of merging Punjab and other provinces with Pakistan then they should listen to this also that Hindus have a right to annex Afghanistan to India so that the boundaries of the Hindu world reach right upto Hinduksuh.

**Hindu Interests and Hindu Mahasabha in Elections**

Veer Savarkar, after this, advised Hindu voters to cast their vote in favour of Hindu Mahasabha candidates only so that the interests of Hindus could be protected.

"So long as the system of communal representation continues in Assemblies, the interests of Hindus cannot be safe there, except when the Hindu members of the assemblies are members of Hindu Mahasabha. Hindu Mahasabha has been founded with the aim that it achieves freedom for Hindustan, maintains its integrity, and obtains share in public services on the basis of proportionate representation and argues for freedom of worship, language and script etc. The future of Hindus demands that the communities and state of India should be based on these principles. Hindu Mahasabha claims that there is no difference between the interests of Hindus and the national interests of Hindustan. We are not prepared to accept an inch less than what is due to us, and are not prepared to give a *ratti* more than due to minorities according to their proportion of population. The Congress, the Forward Bloc and other organisations have committed the sin of violating the principle of this honest nationality. They are lost in the labyrinth of geographical nationality. They have set an ideal before themselves that for fundamental requirements of patriotism, Hindus should be stabbed in the back. In order to keep themselves away from communalism, the Hindu leaders and workers of these institutions feel ashamed of calling themselves Hindus. But they are not ashamed of becoming a member (of Assembly) by participating in communal elections. They play traitor to the service of the community and play a fraud with Hindu voters. If the Congress and the Forward Bloc are ashamed of being the representative organisations of Hindus, then they should not contest elections for Hindu seats only but should try to contest for seats reserved for other communities."

**Making Hindus War-Loving Necessary**

Veer Savarkar expressed the following ideas regarding keeping the Hindus prepared in the face of world war:

"The programme of making Hindus war-loving should continue because the enemy has now reached the doors of India. Therefore, this policy should be implemented fast. The entry of Japan in this war should not affect this policy. Mahasabha believes that England, Germany, Italy, America and Russia are not fighting for others. They are fighting in the interest of their own communities. Therefore, Japan is fighting for its interests. Then India will also do so for its own interests. The interest of our community lies in this. As far as the security of India is concerned, we should co-operate with the efforts of the government of India, join the Army, the Navy and the Air Force in large numbers, and work in ordnance factories."

**Kanpur Session, 1942**

The struggle in Bhagalpur led Hindu Mahasabha into a new self-confidence. It was the biggest achievement of that session. In his speech in the Kanpur session, Veer Savarkar first of all shed light on this achievement. Then he criticized the India tour of the Congress leader Rajagopalachari, presenting his justification of the demand for Pakistan before the people. After this he gave directions to delegates to oppose the Pakistan plan and the repressive policy of the government against the August movement.

**The Achievement of Bhagalpur Struggle**

In Bhagalpur the session has taken the form of a struggle. All Hindus, forgetting their caste, *panth* and other differences, participated in it. Focussing light on it, Veer Savarkar said,

"This year began with the famous unarmed opposition in Bhagalpur. The most important part of this struggle is that it has given in this self-confidence that when an occasion arises, Hindu public even today can prepare a joint front for the defence of *Hindutva* and forget differences of caste, religion community and sect. The spirit of *Hindutva*, for the revival of which Hindu Mahasabha has been working for years, has become so strong due to our good fortune that it can, though neglected for years, not only face anti-

Hindu forces, it can put them down also with its indomitable courage."

A few months after the Bhagalpur front, a meeting of the Akhil Bharatiya Hindu Mahasabha committee was held in Lucknow. Though Muslims demonstrated their riot-prone tendencies, the meeting was successfully completed.

After that in the end of March, Cripps Mission came to India. For years the British government had a feeling that the Congress represented the Hindus, the Muslim League the Muslims, and when both combined they represented Indian nation. But in the meanwhile Hindu Mahasabha established itself as a new political force in such a manner that the British government at the time of the Cripps Mission was forced to acknowledge it as one of the three prominent all-India political institutions. It represented Hindu nation in India.

### Awareness of Hindu Mahasabha

The Congress continuously kept bending before the Muslim pressure: To the extent that it gave a word that if Muslims insisted, it would not oppose the separation/ partition of the provinces. As if the Muslims had not insisted so far to bend the Congress, Shri Rajagopalachari became a symbol of the Pakistani spirit. He toured the whole of India to initiate innocent Hindus into this new 'Pakistan' opinion, and started spreading this epidemic all over. But the members of the Mahasabha were alert and aware. They also went round and washed out the impact created by Rajagopalachari.

### August Movement

All of a sudden thousands of patriotic Congress leaders, including *Mahatma* Gandhi, were assested. This sent a wave of discontent across the country. The government suppressed it. As a result, the atmosphere grew charged and disturbed. Today our Hindu brethren—both Congressi and non-Congressi—have undergone unlimited suffering of house arrest and death, and are still undergoing. They are our brothers. We cannot help appreciating with gratefulness all the suffering they have undergone, inspired by the spirit of patriotism. But we have no sympathy for that unprincipled goondaism which has also gone on side by side.

**To Frustrate the Pakistan Plan**

Veer Savarkar advised Hindus to act upon the following in order to frustrate the Pakistan Plan, in the end of his speech.

(1) Hindus should increase hundred-fold their Hindu militarization movement to join Navy, Air Force, Army and ordnance factories.

(2) Take in your own hands the political powers of the Executive Council of the Viceroy, Cabinet, Legislatures and Defence and other departments.

(3) Do not forget the strength of your organisation in the midst of high slogans.

(4) All the Hindus should unite wherever the rights of Hindus are infringed upon.

(5) Establish branches of Hindu Sabha in all villages and *Talukas*.

(6) If you remove untouchability in the next five years, it would be no less important an achievement than a victory in the battlefield.

When one looks at all these ideas, it becomes clear that Veer Savarkar wanted to see Hindu society as a strong, self-respecting society free from orthodoxy. He always and strongly opposed the partition of India.

**Epilogue**

In preceding chapters, the life story and the philosophy of Veer Savarkar has been described. On considering all this, one naturally comes to this conclusion that freedom fighter Veer Vinayak Damodar Savarkar was such a rare son of *Bharat Mata*, whose entire life was dedicated to his mother- land. He never wavered from his objectives, in spite of running tortures from foreign rulers and narrow and underserved criticism from fellow Indians. Go on struggling. Don't worry for your pains. Don't care for the critics. Don't be afraid of saying and doing what you deem proper. This was his life style.

If you take a bird's eye view of his life right from childhood, it appears that Veer Savarkar was born to struggle for the freedom of his motherland. He never expected respect, fame, post or anything in return of the struggle he undertook to realize his objective. On the contrary, the truth is that the governments of slave and independent India gave him physical and mental tortures only in return of his matchless sacrifice and renunciation.

In history, which is considered an account of what happened in the past, which generally the students study and consider real and true, *is the truth really recorded*? We put a question mark on this element at least when we study the history of India's freedom struggle. The history-writers of this movement have more or less forgotten the revolutionaries who laid down their everything for the freedom of their motherland. To have a difference of opinion is a separate issue, but to draw curtain on the truth is an injustice with history and a moral crime.

If history is visited with an approach to total truth, then the contribution of Veer Savarkar is much more in comparison with that of other leaders who came into power, or those who followed his principles. Generally history appreciates and regards those who are in power. It is unfortunately a bitter truth and India is no exception to it. This is the reason that Veer Savarkar was completely neglected by the government in independent India also. The honours and awards given by our government have remained limited to a particular class only. This element was the reason of Veer Savarkar's neglect.

Veer Savarkar, in reality, considered truth as the highest principle. That was why he always criticized the communal elements and the Congress which followed the policy of appeasement of communal parties and elements. He respected the glorious traditions of the past. Therefore, he thought of maintaining an '*Akhand Hindustan*' in order to protect and develop those glorious traditions. His opponents criticize him for this objective. If he is proved communal, and therefore becomes a butt of criticism, simply because he was a devotee of '*Akhand Bharat*' and a strong opponent of the demand for Pakistan, then those who bent their knees before communal elements and partitioned India by accepting the demand for Pakistan are certainly traitors. It is possible that the sycophant history-writers have described them as gods of India. But truth will always be truth. A day is bound to come when the veil will be lifted from the truth and new students of history study it for finding out the truth. Then Veer Savarkar will get his real, respectable place, and the future generations of India will say, "Veer Savarkar was right. He alone is our ideal." Then will the dream of Savarkar come true.